the LIES we believe

Expanded-Edition!

the LIES we believe

EXPANDED-EDITION!

BOOK ONE

CHRONICLES OF SUICIDE TRILOGY

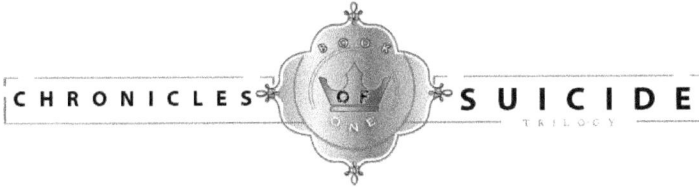

Patricia King

SoS BOOKWORKS

Camden, New York

Patricia King/SoS BookWorks
206 Drought Rd.
Camden, NY/13316
www.scarsofsuicide.com

Publisher's Note: This is a True Account. I have chosen to change some names of actual people in order to protect their privacy. All information used in association with the incidents are of public record and have been documented accordingly.

KJV- NKJV www.Biblehub.com
Book Layout © 2015 BookDesignTemplates.com

The LIES we believe/ Patricia King
CHRONICLES of SUICIDE/ BOOK 1 -- 1st edition

ISBN 978-0-9978793-0-8

TO ALL THOSE WHO LEFT FAR TOO SOON, YOU ARE MISSED
AND YOU ARE LOVED.

CONTENTS

Chapter Three   BLOODline Plumbline

Preface

AMAZON #1 in Kindle Direct Publishing. After I published the 1st teaching element <u>the LIES we believe</u> as an e-book on Amazon KDP, I received many comments and lots of feedback. The e-book parts 1 and 2 made their way to the BESTSELLER lists.

I was so blessed by all the positive, but what stuck with me were those remarks from the people that didn't feel like the book was about suicide.

Well, it is. I took the approach of a teacher, I wanted to share what I had uncovered so that others would gain ground in their situation and struggles. Pointing all towards Jesus.

Essentially these e-books are used as ministry tools, it makes it very convenient to use the Kindle platform to bring materials to people around the globe. I was also able to reduce the price to "free" and sow this into more lives that way during a promotional offer.

I am very excited about all the things that the Lord wants to give to you, by way of revelation knowledge.

-the LIES we believe
-our wounded SOUL
-BLOODline plumbline
PLUS+ BONUS MATERIALS!!

You will receive all three of those e-books in this publication.

I went ahead and compiled the three, which I always intended to do. However, this time around I will share more of my personal story leading up to all the teachings that I have found life changing, the experiences that I want you to grab for your own life. Consider this to be my version of a "Swipe File".

There is a specific and deliberate reasoning for the order that I placed these books. The first three (3) which are sold individually and now as a complied *Expanded Edition*, these are teachings which I believe are fundamental to understanding the next two (2) books in the series.

Titles to come:

> ➤ Scars of SUICIDE (Book 2)
> ➤ The JUDAS Theory (Book 3)

Over the two and 1/2 years that I wrote in my journals and stayed hidden away from the world, I was taken places with the Lord and given information that could no way be found by me, other than by Holy Spirit leading.

If you are new to a relationship with Christ, then you may find what I am saying to be foreign and perhaps a bit confusing. That is precisely why I wrote **the LIES we believe**. The very thing that the enemy does is deceive us. Just as it happened to Adam & Eve in the Holy Garden so long ago.

Same trick, new audience.

Most of my story is taken straight from my journals. I wanted to be authentic and *keep it real*. You deserve the truth. Isn't that, after all what you came looking for? It would be wrong to give you the fluffy watered down version.

Reading it might be difficult, I know that going back over it was very taxing for me, at times. Please grant me grace to tell my story of living through multiple suicides. Realizing, many individuals will never know the searing pain of suicide but every type of people will read a book like this.

No one ever asks for a life filled with heartache, we do ask for ways to cope. Letting my story out allows me to do much more than cope, I have healed through the journaling and I have seen the Hand of God reach out to comfort me.

This is a TRUE ACCOUNT. I will be sharing details of the incidents when I write about those days.

It is my life.

Taking all things into consideration and placing appropriate boundaries, I will open up about three suicides that I have lived through. I only have two options before me, sit down and be quiet which allows the enemy to keep stomping around and tearing through lives with this destruction. Option 2 is that I share what I have found and pray that as many people as the Lord brings to read this will find the *doors* in their own lives and most importantly find the way to shut those entry points once and for all.

If you were to search a bookstore for "Rare" books that do not even have an ISBN # you will find my story in two editions of a testimony book written in 2008 & 2011. My story was tucked in, amongst many others and the books were printed for ministry work in the mission fields, globally. Last that I knew it had gone to over 100 Nations and been translated to 6 languages. I never thought this even possible. My story was now available for individuals that spoke Haitian, French **Creole** and Pakistani Urdu, along with other languages that I have never seen in print. It was humbling and I believed that I had completed what the Lord asked of me.

I guess I felt *that* was adequate enough for my story to be told. I have forgiven those who hurt me and I have moved into ministry work with my Lord and Savior Jesus.

My days are spent praying with others; as the Lord sends individuals into my life. Working through deep issues of the heart that can be healed with love, patience to care and of course prayer ministry. This is accomplished through church (altar ministry) or through the Internet and the myriad of tools now available to this generation.

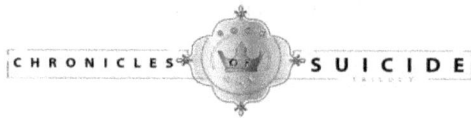

The events within CHRONICLES of SUICIDE did in fact take place and I hope to clearly show you what I chose to do in order to survive it all. For I tell you true, the devil surely came to steal/ kill and destroy me.

Staying alive and surviving the darkest times when they come, is the only option that I support.

It is never okay to take your own life. This statement is not merely an opinion. Let me say it again.

It is never okay to take your own life.

That being said, if you feel like you may hurt yourself in any way, please call this **HOTLINE** and ask for the help they have made available. Asking for help does not make you weak, it makes you **brave.**

There are many people who care about you, even if you do not feel like it right now. The world needs you, that is why you are here; for such a time as this. **1-800 273-8255**

NATIONAL
SUICIDE
PREVENTION
LIFELINE
1-800-273-TALK (8255)
suicidepreventionlifeline.org

CHAPTER ONE

The LIES We Believe

As Believers in Christ, the only word we ever need take heed of is the Holy Bible. Even if we know it is true how can we walk it out on a daily journey of faith? Too often the lies we believe were planted long ago, we might not know it is even a 'lie' we may just think it is correct because we heard it from a trusted source.

How does this happen, and what can we do about it now? We have all dealt with lying, no one really likes being lied to or being called a liar. So, how is it then that so many of us find ourselves ensnared in the lies that bind us to the enemy of our soul? The short answer is ignorance.

Hold on! I am not saying that anyone is stupid, I am saying that what we don't know, can hurt us. Isaiah tells us that people perish for lack of knowledge, it takes knowledge and discernment to gain vision. Forward thinking, planning and dreaming. You won't be doing any of these things if you are bound up in bitterness or unforgiveness. If you have a boat anchor of anger dragging you down, it becomes terribly difficult to soar in the things of God. Most, if given a choice, would not opt in for bondage, but to soar like eagles. If we were all soaring and roaring for the Lord, the devil would be out of commission. However, just one glance at the condition of the world and you see, we [the people] have gotten ourselves into quite a bind. Now what?

I am going to show you just that, and I pray you will begin to see the lies from truth in your own life, know that when you do, it is a gift from God and He will help you change what needs changing, or mend what has been broken. That is what the love of God does for His children. I am living proof.

My heart had been broken. Not just a little crack, but shattered. It was fragile to begin with, chipped up and beat down from many years of disappointments and from what seemed like a constant onslaught of sucker punches and death. I teetered back and forth, not ever quite making it to that place of peace I would read about... the one that passes all understanding. Even after I had been walking with Jesus for many years, I suffered another death blow to my own soul, years of lies had taken away someone very dear to me.

People have Limits

In the many years of prayer ministry spanning over several states (as the Lord led me) from Alaska to New York, I have found that people are people wherever you go, and that these individuals have limits of what they can handle. This is because the topic of suicide reaches into all of us, it pierces and it pokes about looking for weaknesses. To think on it and stare it in the face, we quickly recognize that we are now looking at our own mortality. And this frightens us.

If hindsight is 20/20 then that certainly applies here. Most of the times that I have shared anything personal, it was only because the subject came up in conversation. As a rule I do not deliberately share my past and would consider myself to be somewhat protective in this area. I use the word protective, because I have found that too many times judgment has flowed my way, when I do share. Knowing this you might well imagine how much anxiety could well up inside when the Good Lord asked me to be 'transparent' and begin to deal with shame/guilt/rejection and make them my footstool. I can tell you this is an ongoing process and although I have gained tremendous victory in so many areas, there are times that the old creeper comes back, trying to build walls and close off access.

Let me interject here that God knows what He is doing.
He knows how to lovingly guide us through the land mines of our heart and maneuver us to success IN Him.
So, with the small and timid steps of a newborn I began to open up. Gradually- *because* people have limits and that goes for both sides of the conversation.
Usually when I am asked a question or receive a comment like

"How can you even smile?" or "Wow, you should be a serial killer after all that." This is when I know, that at this point the individual I am speaking with has heard enough. Those kinds of statements indicate that they are trying to process the information, and grasp what they have heard. This individual has hit their limit. To go on any further would just be like 'gossip' and would bring more glory to the devil than it would to the Lord Jesus Christ.

Anyone can go on and on about tragic events, but consider this first, is the listener going to be *blessed* by what you share? Is there any reason to get into every last one of the gory details? A little can go a long way, and if the conversation leads to a deeper place I will go there too.

It might be best explained this way, and I have fondly named it the 'gawker syndrome'. Have you ever driven by an auto accident and found yourself unable to look away? There are ambulance and fire-trucks in the road, your lane has gone from two down to one, and you're moving at less than 10 mph. You might even begin to pray for those involved, but can you look away as you pass the wreckage? I think it is human nature to look and I am not pointing fingers, I am making a point. More often than not, we do look to see what we can see, as you hope against hope that there won't be anything showing. Those, who were involved in the accident that wait on the shoulder of the road avoid the unrelenting gaze, they don't really want to share the details of what just happened because they are still too shook up. The gawker still gawks because they just can't look away. Yes, these are the sort of stares I have received during moments of sharing my life story. When that look appears on the listeners face I know they have reached their limit to hear what I am sharing. It's the Lord's wisdom that has brought me this understanding, and it is sound wisdom.

Only share a % percentage of the story, only give the necessary de-tails. As the years have gone by, it becomes easier to identify the gawker from the genuine. The genuine are connecting and they see themselves in the details, they want (or need) to know that this nightmare story has a happy ending.

They need to know that they too can be saved from misery and heartache. Those are the individuals that I try to share my story with, to look back as I re-tell the events and realize there were 100's of times that I should have died in what I was doing, but in some strange twist, here I am- alive and searching for the right words to express the gratitude in my heart, even if it is difficult to find the 'language'.

Jesus is the only one that can handle all the times we are so needy. Putting too much on others comes from a need to be heard. There is a time and a place for the hearing & the telling.

Let me use a married couple for my example. Every person comes to the Lord with their own baggage. It is the same in a marriage, we become one flesh, but we still have our own baggage to deal with. If one 1/2 of the marriage equation relies on the other for every single problem, then they will place too much on their spouse. I am not talking about topics such as, what to have for dinner.

I am referring to deep emotional issues. Abandonment, rejection, depression, or fears that are rooted in childhood. Your spouse may not even be equipped to deal with it all; but expecting them to "fix" all of it, you may actually push them away. Which then triggers those other emotions (not yet healed) rejection etc. What a cycle! My answer for this is to share only what is needful (because honesty is vital) and to give the rest over to the foot of the cross.

Jesus actually wants to carry our baggage and He is well able to trade yokes with you.

That being said, and even though I felt like I would be complaining or dredging up past incidents, I am going to open up and share some of my "issues" in this Expanded Edition of Book 1. It seems that I am consistently asked to be transparent. My testimony will not be lopsided by only sharing the good that the Lord has done for me. I will share a little about what I went through for Him to even need to rescue me so completely, from the pit of hell and even from myself at times.

My most painful memories will be shared, it is the very substance of what led up to my own attempt at suicide. I have seen groups on FB that are dedicated to suicide survivors and the like. They will not post your comment if you mention anything about the way that a person died. Not the weapon or the details in anyway. This is not my approach, dodging and hiding are no longer my way, I join the groups that let people freely share and invite open discussions of their pain, in order to heal, for there is no joy found in gossip.

Remember when Robin Williams took his life? Didn't we want to know the why of it? Didn't we wonder if it was overdose or a hanging? I do not believe we think of these questions to be morbid. It is impossible to hear of a suicide and not to ask *how?* I have found connections in the Spiritual Realms that clearly show how "doors" are opened and that these same doors can be closed. Remember Whitney Houston and her death? Now, if you do not know the story, you can goggle it. Look into her daughter Bobbi's death as well. These things are public record, and you will find that they died in a very similar manner. So many overlapping details, that you cannot ignore it.

Here is the question I am asked most often
"How did you get through that?" And of course...
"Why?"
"Why did it happen?" Which is immediately followed by "How?"

You too, have a need for answers or you would not be here. Perhaps you are wondering if you are always going to be trapped in this place of painful memories and the repeating sounds, sights and thoughts which hold you captive in the small hours of the night....

You catch yourself wondering things like, is this just the way life is going to be now. Will I ever be free of this torment?

I will do my best to tackle all of these questions, for they were also upon my heart and the very reason I went so deep into the Word of God and lived only (for a season) to do nothing else but satisfy my need for answers.

The Lord was very gracious and patient with me. He provided all I needed along the way.

I found a new *walk in the Lord*, a new way to approach problems of life. **I had to go beyond where I once was, in order to get where I was now going.**

This takes courage and perseverance. Two things I worked on *while* I grew In Jesus.

That is fundamental; to realize that you do not wait until you get it all figured out in order to begin. You just begin!

Wrestling for the Blessing

We do not always wrestle the Lord for our blessing, as Jacob did. In fact there are many times that we wrestle the principalities and powers, along with darkness of this age. Remember the fight is not against flesh and blood, although the arena is located within our flesh and along our bloodlines.

Depression is the last Hoorah before
the dance of death

My struggle with depression did not go on for years and it took many twists and turns. No less than three (3) times can I attest to wrestling with depression. I will briefly share my journey, it is important for me to note here that I am extremely grateful and very sure that Jesus was the One who stepped in between myself and the oppression of depression, showing Himself mighty as He spread His arms —standing between me and the devil and said "No, you cannot go any further." I shall never forget the humbling experience of it, nor the safety of peeking over His shoulder as the enemy retreated.

This particular event occurred somewhere in the middle of the two suicides, just to give you a time line and a perspective of the battle, as an onlooker.

I have a "Seer" gift. I never knew what it was until after I began to read the Bible, many pivotal points came as I read and read, submersing myself into the WORD, as it wound itself / *Himself* deeper into the fabric of my DNA. The only reason I bring this up, is because to tell my story I will have to share the things I "saw" and this will certainly seem strange to any that do not have this type of gifting, or the Biblical background to discern what was taking place.

I have been told that I am an empath (which is a word used by people that don't know about seer gifts) I have been called a prophetess and even a mystic. There were a couple occasions where I was asked if I was a medium (that one is for talking to the dead, which I have no desire to do). So how do I know, which one it is? The Lord told me, He said "You will be like Samuel."

Many years earlier, I remembered that the Books of 1&2 Samuel helped me to work out my heartaches from my teenage years, the Bible put words to my feelings and I was able to then give those painful times over to Jesus. However it took an act of God to reveal the scripture to me in ~ 1Chronicles 29:29.

"Now the acts of David the king, from the first to the last, behold, they are written in the book of Samuel the seer, and in the book of Nathan the prophet, and in the book of Gad the seer."

There are 66 books in the Bible, written by 44 authors. The books of Nathan and Gad never made it into the KJV. It is no surprise that the Lord knew this when He said to me "You will be like Samuel."

I have only come to understand these things in the past 8 years (since about 2007) when I purposefully and deliberately sought to know what was happening all through my life with these visions and what could I do to either stop it or learn to live with it.

At that time it hadn't occurred to me that I might actually be able to use this gifting to help myself or others.

The "Dark Blanket"

There are two ways that I see depression. One is a very large and dark blanket (as in the size of a room, so that the shadow of it would block out all light.) The second is a cavernous hole in the ground, yawning and growling from deep within its throat. The pit calls and beckons, it whispers lies and plays on emotions that desire peace, an escape from the torment of dread and despair.

Both are evil and derive their power from hell's torment, the same as can be found in the gnashing of teeth (which I always believed was the nagging torment of regret, that picks away your flesh and your mind because you can't or won't forgive, picking and chewing at you until it has eaten you up.) Forgiving is one powerful way to stop the gnashing of regret.

The first time I can recall the "Dark Blanket" was after my first husband David took his own life, he died right in front of the police, gunshot wound to the head. He passed away in the morning around 9:00am. By that evening, the "urge" to return to the place of his death was so strong, that my friend had to physically restrain me from leaving her house. It was "calling" me and I am 100% certain that if I had returned to our home where he died only 12 hours earlier, I could have ended my own life too.

Let me back up a few steps.

On the morning of David's death, it was already in his mind to do what he did. I carried years of guilt around because I didn't see it coming and I was his *wife*. It's true that he had changed and become different, but I couldn't place my finger on it, the behavior that he displayed can now be looked back upon and yes, I could say this or that was a warning sign.

Hindsight has been an arduous teacher.

Skipping over many moments from that awful day and just touching the points that are relevant here. We were arguing, *again*. It was becoming a regular thing. I was not okay with his behavior and I was pushing for a change.

One of the last things I ever said to him was "We need to go to counseling!"

His reply "I'd rather die than go to counseling."

How was I supposed to know that statement was so true? How many times does someone yell out in anger, only to be venting a frustration?

I proceeded with the morning routines, my daughter went into the bathtub.

He took our son to school. They had an argument too, but I wouldn't find out about that until a while later (when my son also revealed to me that he believed his dad died because of their fight).

I was not paying much attention to David when he returned, he went into our room which was down the hall from the living room and to the right around the corner. He began calling me, it was a strange high-pitch voice and it made the hair on the back of my neck stand up. Something inside me said not to follow, I kind of instinctively knew that he was going to hurt me if I went over by him.

That didn't matter, he came out to the kitchen and he had his hunting rifle with him. I can't remember what he kept saying in that strange voice, I tried to get away from him and ran around the table, headed for the door but he stopped me and forced me up against the window he held a gun to my face and repeatedly pulled the trigger.

Click- click-click....

Time after time the bullets did not fire. He left the house, only to return with new bullets, just purchased a few miles down the road. While he was gone I placed the 911 call. I explained that he was going to drive right up onto the lawn and proceed to kill me. They came over immediately, but laughed off everything that I told them. I must have looked like a maniac because nobody was taking me serious. You know the scene in *Terminator* where the main character is locked up at an asylum and she is desperately trying to get people to listen to her, but nobody will. That was me, trapped in a weird place with no way to get through to the only help I had. The report was taken down and the police left.

When he came back, he drove right up on to the lawn as I saw in my mind's eye. The exact spot! I was on the phone with the school, by this time everything inside me was screaming that something bad was about to happen and I scrambled to stop the events as they unfolded. I was in the process of explaining to the school that he had a gun and to keep my 10 year old (Justin) in the school, because I feared he could become a hostage. I had no idea where he had gone to or when he would return.

David never exited the vehicle. I looked out the window, my husband's body was sitting in the truck looking at the house but what starred back at me, was no longer my husband. His eyes were completely black, just deep holes in his head. Terror shot through me as I turned once to see that the police were in the driveway with their guns drawn and held on the top of the squad cars, two of them pointed on the truck, aimed at him. Time was in slow motion, every sense was heightened. I turned back to David, he was placing the shot gun in his mouth. I screamed "NO!" and I turned toward the hallway and ran. I never heard the gun shot, and the school was still on the phone!

This is the fraction of a second, that instance where you have no time to formulate a plan. I remember thinking "No" you will not put that image into my head, seeing you die. "No" as in don't do this!! And "NO!" this cannot happen.

But it did happen and the days and months which followed were dark indeed. His family insisted that I had murdered him. They repeatedly called my local police and the detective who was on the case. He contacted me once to warn me what was happening, he told me that no matter what he said to them from the events that morning they were still convinced that I did it. He was concerned for my safety. A map of the shooting was placed in the paper and many people drove by slowly to see what they could see. I was very vulnerable and decided to sell the house and move away.

One more minute later, just one more minute and the police would have been gone and I would be deceased as well. The detectives and years later my pastor (who was the officer on duty to talk down a suicidal shooter) told me that usually the person kills everyone in the family and then ends their own life.

So, my daughter is **living in the space of Grace as well.**

I met David when I was 14, and we were together until he passed 16 years later. He suffered from untreated depression. He died only 5 months after his 34th birthday. He left his two children behind and a gaping wound in our lives that to this day has not healed in all that were affected. He has been gone 17 years now in November as I write this in the year 2015. Some things you just never can forget. I became a widow at the age of 30, I was left to raise a 10 year old boy and a 5 year old girl all by myself.

As I mentioned earlier that I felt the strangest urge to return to the house where he took his life. I had many encounters with an evil presence after he died. I was fearful of it, yet I also knew that I did not have to "agree" with it, nor allow it to stay.

One time, the "Dark Blanket" hovered over me, and I actually felt its weight. There was a kind of suggested relief from my pain & grief if I chose to have it cover me.

The thing spoke to me, I can't explain it any better than that, and it said "Can I cover you?"

Isn't that strange, for it to ask would mean it needed permission-from me, and I told it "NO."

Another time, as I sat on my bedroom floor sobbing, overcome by my own forms of sorrow mixed with self-hatred, I sensed (felt) something standing behind me. In another realm, I saw a transparent figure of a woman I think, all skin and bones floating there like a fog or a cloud like substance, the face was a skull and had no features, but the hair was long, white, cloud- like moving as if under water. Again I told it to leave me alone. The certainty that if I turned around, I would see it; disturbed me enough not to turn around.

Moments later, Justin came in and asked me what I was crying about, and he said he never wanted to hear me cry like that again because it scared him. I made a decision that day to keep the ugly business of grieving from Justin (he turned 11 years old, one month after his father died) and his sister turned 5 the day before his death. We began the process of grieving in silence. A mistake I will have to live with, but will not repeat a second time.

Many things transpired and life changed over and over during the next 7 years. I was remarried and living in Alaska when depression came again to ask the question. "Can I cover you?" Only this time it did not ask me, it spoke directly to my husband Michael. The short version of the story is that we were packing up to leave Alaska and I was pretty upset you could even say I was distraught.

During a crying episode, while packing this "thing" whatever it was asked my husband "Can I get her?" and thankfully he said "No." He told me later that he was pretty mad at me, of course we were not in harmony about the move and the way Justin left and the chaos in the house was escalating. Two babies in diapers, moving and Michael had been working up on the slope (the Alaskan pipeline which kept him away for weeks at a time) Needless to say there was tension. I did not want to return to the place where David (my 1st husband) had taken his own life. I was being forced to face head on the shame and sorrow that I moved away from.

Justin had left Alaska 3 months after his 17th birthday. He said his grandparents (paternal) bought a round trip ticket for him. I reluctantly agreed to all of it. Someone else took him to the airport, I never got to say good bye.

His grandparents fought me on the issue of bringing him home. The law said he was old enough to stay there in Michigan if he wanted to. I packed everyone up and returned to the lower 48. I knew that I would not see him again if I remained living with such a vast distance between us.

The months that followed our coming back to the town where David died were nearly too much for me to bear. I was saved by this time and water baptized and living for the Lord.

Things should be easy right? Life got tangled up in the past again. I had gained so much freedom while in Alaska, I went through deep prayer ministry, focused on removing those burdens I carried for so long after the death of my first husband. It became my determined goal to know Christ and to be deliberate about my future. As I studied and grew in understanding, I was becoming better equipped to fight the enemy that poked at me all the time.

I even went through the training offered by the church to become a Biblical counselor, aiding others in prayer ministry. I attended everything I could make it too, including the Global Awakening by Randy Clark that was held at the Alaska State fair grounds. Bill Johnson and Neil Lozano were also Pastors/leaders there. Four days after completing my specialized training through the church, we pulled out of the most beautiful place I have ever lived. My heart broke.

I had endless reasons to stay in Alaska, but my son left and that was the deciding factor. Even though he was 17, there were still areas of his life that we knew better than his grandparents ever could, I knew he still needed us and I wanted to be available when he realized it. For now, I rationalized that living with them would be the best way to get to know his father. Justin was water baptized in Eagle River while we lived in Alaska. He too was growing in the Lord. I wanted to remain secure in that surety, and let him be in the Hands that created Him.

Justin was enrolled in High School, which as it turns out, was the same High School that his father and I graduated from. Now he was living in the town where I went through foster care. More of the past surfaced and people whom I lost touch with, were now getting to know my boy. Justin came to visit us immediately when we moved back into the house I bought when his father died. A place for us to start over. This was located 45 minutes from Chicago. Five (5) hours from his grandparents' home in Northern Michigan. We saw Justin for all major Holidays, his birthday landed 2 days after Christmas and it was wonderful to have him home with us. He was a joy to be around.

As time wore on, I slipped deeper into the pit. I could see it so clearly, that gaping hole. I wanted to stop feeling the way I did. Sadness has a way of turning into despair, and despair has a heavy thickness to it that doesn't shake off easily. I slept a lot, and I tried to keep up with normal routines. Bible studies went on for hours, I would be transported away, and while I was in the Spirit I found peace. The trouble is, you can't live your life from that place and I would have to return to my regularly scheduled program, which these days was sadness. I was sad and "low" I could feel it, like a foreign object sucking the life out of me.

Going to church helped a great deal. While at home, I wrestled with my own demons, guilt and fear were two of them. I felt shame as well. Things I thought I had overcome, still they clung to me. I would lay on my Bible and repeat scripture, I slept with it under my pillow, and I wore the thing right out. After a while even a heavy cover could not keep it in tact. The strangest parallel world developed. During my wrestling with depression I felt like I didn't know how to get to the other side, I didn't know how to kick it in the teeth and get free of it. However, when I prayed for others and *their* freedom, mighty works were happening in the Name of Jesus.

Within 3 months of being in this new church, I was asked to consider leading the prayer ministry, to work alongside others at the altar and to teach a class on Biblical Freedom. If you were to ask me today, I would just say that the Lord has a sense of humor!

What Jesus opened up to me, were avenues (should I chose to take them) of healing. I was known in the church as the "Woman who did healing and deliverance" Most didn't even know my name or where I came from. The Pastor (from the hostage squad at David's death) and his wife kept me close and watched over me, every time the enemy pulled me back, they would offer room for advancement in the Kingdom. In the class that I taught, most of the attendees were women and the regular ones to come in were wives of the other leaders and Pastors in the church. So, I can confidently say that they would have discernment about what I was teaching and what the Lord was continually showing me. This was the church that the visions were the strongest and the prophetic realms became clearer. I no longer could deny what was happening and I could not run from it, so I learned to embrace the "Seer" gift and grow in it too.

Learning by *"Experiencing Jesus"* was the way that the Holy Spirit taught me. I would cry out, and He would come in and teach me to fight the enemy by using the WORD (which Holy Spirit opened up understanding to) and then the power of God would come whooshing in to save me when I was over run.

The more the enemy roared at me, the bigger Jesus showed up. I grew in trust and my faith with confidence were exploding in me and around me. I fought so many spirits of darkness during this time, not only what was buried in me, but things that were lurking around other's lives too, even a Jezebel spirit that was present in the leadership at the church. Don't read too much into this because the spirit of religion is in many churches today, along with lust and pride and jealousy.

God's people are not perfect, they are *made* perfect through Christ and that is by the grace of God, not by people or their works. I can rest in knowing that I do not have to have it all figured out in order to approach the throne of Grace. I come to God in the condition I am in, He does the real work in me to bring up or pull out what does not belong.

My depression "issue" or condition, was against the works of the Healing Cross, so I knew it didn't belong and that it would have to bend to the will of God. I kept fighting / praying / worshiping / believing / hoping for the power of Jesus to come and rescue me. He was my only Hope.

Push came to shove one day and I broke down, going against what I believed in order to do what those around me thought best. I went to the doctor to get medication for the depression. I felt weak and helpless, not knowing how to get past this problem. We were at least 6 months into it. I stated in the beginning of my story it was less than a year, but it was an exhausting fight, that raged day and night to wear me down and fill me with hopelessness.

Every single time I took the medication, I prayed over it. Somewhere down inside me I knew I didn't want this to be my future, who does right? So, I would no sooner take the pill and then zap, I would feel the transmitters in my brain firing off. I can't explain it any better, I could feel the medication electrifying my brain, and it hurt! After a very short time, less than 3 weeks I had this revelation. It was more like remembering something I had heard along the way. There was a woman who would get terrible headaches from wearing her glasses and when she went to the eye doctor he told her that the headaches were because she no longer needed the glasses, she was healed and received corrected vision!

I knew that this was what I now faced, I was so sure of it that I stopped taking the medication. Just like that, and it was over. I no longer needed the medication, and the weight was lifted. I came out of the depression. I would state, without reservation that it was a miracle and that all of the heaviness fell away. It was just myself and the Lord, in the room that I prayed in all the time. That is why I know Jesus showed up and He did the kicking, which sent the devil straight on out. I received my healing and it was glorious! As a side note, I recommend that you ask a doctor before discontinuing any medication.

My healing experiences with Jesus are in the hundreds and climbing. Every time I step out of that proverbial boat, He is ready to catch me when I stumble. There isn't any distance He won't go to get those that He loves, and I am telling you that Jesus loves all.

Once more in 2012, I briefly saw that pit, and heard the beaconing to come in. Only this time I was not just living for the Lord, I was fully running the race. I went to sleep with peace on my heart and was awaken that night with a phone call that my beautiful Justin age 22 had taken his life, just as his father did 13 years earlier. He died in his grandparent's driveway as they looked on.

I write about all of this tragedy in the *Chronicles of Suicide*; **Scars of Suicide** -Book 2. Justin fought depression, and he also fought the ups and downs of having type 1 insulin dependent diabetes. In the 5 years that he lived away from us, the world unraveled his faith, in people, in himself and I believe even in God and the power of His Name to heal.

In the end he only believed the lies that were fed to him. I wish he would have reached out to us and allowed us to bring him back home.

He died with a loss of hope and basically homeless. His grandparents promised to love him and to provide a home for him. In my heart, I do not feel they loved him unconditionally as only the Lord can truly do anyway.

So, there is nothing left to do except release them and turn it *all* over to Father God. I have forgiven them and I hope that they can forgive me too for all the ways they feel I let others down. In some strange way I hoped against all odds that they could see how the deaths were similar and that when their son died next to my driveway, there just was no way for me to stop the actions set in motion. The police had guns drawn on him, but could not fire if he didn't point it at them. Even the police were saying they couldn't stop him. Yet, when my son died in their driveway and they were outside with him, they too could not move faster than a speeding bullet and so we all lost our precious boys when they took every decision out of our hands in a moment's notice.

This war isn't fought nor won with hatred.

It is a victory in love
-when love triumphs at the foot of the cross

I truly want peace for them and for no more destruction to come into their lives. Whenever they come to my mind, I place them in the hands of Jesus.

This is where I started looking at the lies. I wasn't the only one who was baffled by the events that took place so suddenly one unassuming morning in late November of 1999 and then again in October of 2012.

Both of these men were very intelligent, hardworking and interested in a bright future.

David was the kind of guy you went to for answers, he knew a lot of things about many subjects. He was great with money and the mechanics side of antique cars. He worked at a tool and die company before going to college in Chicago and then getting a salaried position with a top name Medical company. He serviced MRI machines and various other X-Ray based equipment. He was an engineer, an absolute whiz with numbers. His son Justin held that same aptitude for math.

How then does such a high level thinker become a person that nobody recognizes? How does he go from being on top of the world, to the bottom of a pit filled with depression and death?

David was the 5th person in his family (maternal side) to die by suicide in a 25 year period. If there were more I do not know of it. I cannot divulge those details here, for it is not my place to bring those to light. Our Justin was the 6th.

I know of one person on my (paternal side) that died by suicide. One morning I was awakened with enlightening information from the Lord about that incident. The young woman who died was only 16, as it turns out she is my aunt and they called her Patsy, but her Christian name was Patricia she (is my name sake). The story I was told all my life about Patsy was a very sad tale indeed. She was damaged during child birth, something about the forceps used in delivery. As the story went, and I heard it from more than one individual, she was extremely strong and prone to violent fits of uncontrolled rage. My grandparents feared for the safety of the other children. I even heard about how she threw my father down some stairs once. What was brought to my attention in a morning dream was about Patsy's death. I guess I wasn't thinking very much about it but since I was writing these books on the subject of suicide, I believe the Lord brought it up for me to take into account. What I had forgotten from so long ago was that....Patsy hung herself in a strait jacket. She died by suicide, regardless of her state of mind. The information given to me when I was less than 12 years old, did not surface again until over 35 years later.

These things did not go un-noticed by me, I began to research the deaths and then the attempts made. When I counted up all of them, including the ones I have just mentioned, I found the number to be 24. From both sides of the family. This does not include multiple attempts by any individual. When I added those who shared with me after the events took place, the number rose to over 40. That is too high of a number to ignore that there is a crisis in my family and in the population of the world!

You might not believe in generational curses; you might want to rethink your position.

You see, David had a different truth than those around him. I can say that because to say the opposite is to agree that when a person takes their own life, they would be correct in doing so. But of course they are Not correct or remotely on the right path.

I conclude that he bought into another set of realities. The ones that made him out to be worthless and useless. Where he thought he was not enough. He wrestled the lust of the flesh and the pride of life. The twisted truth that said, you should be removed from the face of the earth. The lying whispers, sent by the father of lies; lies brought up straight from hell.

The devil comes in on any coat tail that he can, pride is a big one. There can be fear and jealousy too, even anger and hatred can unlock an entry. Once inside, the enemy quickly begins to pick at your thoughts and emotions. Shooting his flaming arrows at you relentlessly. Those arrows have words written upon them. Words like loser, failure, and stupid, moron, disgusting or pathetic.

You might be able to deflect some of those arrows and maybe even keep on your mask for a while longer. But soon enough you begin to pick up the arrows, and more of them come. You begin to form your own labels like rejected, unwanted or unloved. You take these labels on one by one. This brings them into your soul and once they get rooted, it will take the power of God to remove them.

David always seemed to have an inferiority complex, one that he covered with quick witted comments to make the rest of us feel dumb. All the while, he hoped that he would not be found out, or it be discovered that he didn't really think all that fondly of himself. As his wife I saw past that facade. I enjoyed his mind and our conversations. He was a dreamer and an artist. He didn't need to try so hard to shine when the audience left. He would tinker on his cars and for the most part, there were lots of quiet evenings. But then the race day would come and we were pushed to the back ground.

The racing, drinking and strip clubs were now all his focus was on. I don't understand the mentality that people slide into when they try to re-live their glory days.

I began to despise the cars. The women that I knew were not faithful to their own husbands. Men in this group were not faithful to their wives.

He told me that part but he also tried to keep reassuring me that he was not doing those things.

In my heart I knew better. I wanted to believe the lie that if I loved him enough and the children and I were steadfast, he would come around, not needing that other life to fill a void in his heart.

Human love is limited, where God's love is limitless. I could never be all he needed, that is a place for the great I AM to fill. My ignorance in this was not a blissful state to be in.

Coming Into Focus

I began long ago with a determined search for answers, each time I was led straight back to my own heart. The frustration became unbearable, for you see it was within my own choices (made each day) that the answers began to reveal themselves.

"Who can understand his errors? Cleanse me from my secret faults." -Psalms 19:12

Repeatedly I returned, as this mess of lies took some time to unravel. I discovered many corrupt thought patterns and nearly everything that could go wrong, had gone wrong. Jesus sure had His hands full with me!

Please, understand that I have been wrecked and destroyed, nearly to my own demise from the lies that I believed. Personally, the Spirit of Suicide has touched my life many times over, until it seemed that I may actually be being 'stalked' by the unseen forces which kept colliding with my life. My search, led me to Jesus and He then introduced me to me. I didn't like what I saw.

This is when life began to come into focus. After what seemed like an eternity to me, little things around me began to come into focus, then gradually "I" began to come into focus. Years of sifting myself through the Word of God and learning about humility and true love from Jesus continually washing over me, the layers of grime began to peel away. The changes had been happening all along but I didn't notice. Tucked away in my heart, I kept the offenses written against me. After all, it was easier to believe the lies, than to accept the truth and free myself from prison. I'm a work in progress.

Three very important areas of each one's lives are constantly under attack. Each individual is on their own sojourn moving through life. As a Christian we are each called to walk out our own Salvation. Many issues are common to man and we all suffer from the condition and the position of being human. Prone to sin. The highest concentration of attacks on people, whether saved or un-saved are in these areas.

Identity, Authority, and Responsibility. In that order. I will shed a bit of light on each area and expose a few of the lies that lurk around in each position of our lives. But first it will be beneficial to lay some foundation. Stick around, you might be surprised what you learn and keep this thought tucked away, knowledge is power. I want you to be powerful, specifically empowered by the Spirit of God. –*elaion*.

What Is Seen & What Is Unseen

Identity. Let's start here, because that is usually where the trouble starts. We have the best example of Jesus addressing the issues of Who He is, as He takes on the devil, out in the wilderness. Luke 4:1-13, reading these passages from your bible can help you understand a whole lot about identity. You see, Jesus knew Who He was, Is and Is yet to become. The lies of the devil did not sweep Him up, nor did they confuse Him for even a second. God's children however, suffer from a terrible identity crisis. When you do not know who you are, or even to whom it is that you belong, how then will you take up your sword? What would you stand for? From what position do you gain your victory?

Do you realize that just because something seems true to you, does not make it a truth in real terms, only when it lines up with the Word of God can you be sure that it is truth. So, two things can be happening simultaneously here. Your perceived truth; because it is true to you, you're going to live your life from that position, thereby perpetuating the (lie) as if it were truth. Second, in the Spirit Realm (which is parallel to our seen realm) the Truth is trying to break forth in your life, which is Jesus; The way, the truth and the life.

I can give you an example from my own life. I had an extreme distrust for authority. (My lie) that I lived from, insisted that anyone in authority would abuse their position. Primarily any male figure. This to me meant that men and most definitely 'father figures' couldn't be trusted. The lie I perpetuated and lived from was that because of what I had lived through and what brought me to foster care, group homes and eventually being set out on my own at the age of 16, is that men in authority were evil. Now, how do you think this lie affected every relationship there after? How could I trust anyone? From my experience, that the foster homes and group homes were filled with men that couldn't keep their hands to themselves and that time and again the girls in the homes were not protected. I didn't feel safe, and I sure didn't feel loved.

All the while, in the spirit realm, Jesus was trying to break through to me and reveal His love which is a representation of Father God's love. I had two things happening at the same time and both were truth, even though one was really a lie.

(My perception was only truth to me, not biblically sound.) Father God is the ultimate authority, the Sovereign Lord, but I was terrified to trust even one more person with my mangled heart. I would eventually come to know Abba as my daddy, and allow Him to bring me to a place of forgiveness to each time I had been betrayed. It took a while, but He is patient.

More examples come from the beginning of the good book, to read Genesis, several times can uncover the unseen realms rather nicely. Each time I go through it, I am shown another amazing situation. We are going in a different direction now, for the purpose of this study. The lies, and who the father of those lies would be. Knowledge is power. We are after the kind that is written on the heart, not in the head.

"The thief comes, only to steal, kill and destroy." –John 10:10

There isn't much of a stretch to discern that suicide is linked to the Spirit of Death, making this connection should be easy enough.

The question then becomes; where does this spirit originate and what can we [the people] do?

Even if suicide isn't the issue in your life and you never thought things like, "The world would be a better place without me in it." Or "Who would notice if I died?" "Who would care?" "I don't amount to much anyway, so what's the point?" Where you ever told, as I was "I wish you were never born?" Be careful, because any words of death spoken over your life can open doors that the devil will slink right on through when you aren't looking and then on that dread filled day when times are hard, he will begin the process of un-raveling what you know about yourself that is good and reflects God.

I will try my best to explain what has been revealed to me. To begin let me bring something to your attention, I really don't want you to miss this, so I will start here and move into the point I am making. God the Father, Jesus the Son and the Holy Spirit all three have many characteristics and all 3 have many names by which [we] his children can call Him. They are 3 but still They are One.

This point is made clear in Genesis 1:26 you can look it up when you have time. Each characteristic and each name were derived from the nature by which the Trinity functions as we know them from the Bible or even presently, in your life. My best example is this, if you are sick you would pray or 'Call upon' The Lord Who Heals- Yahweh Rophe to God YHWH, this being the same God I would call ELOHIM – The Creator or the God Most High -- EL ELYON. Still further I can pray to Jesus – YESHUA-the Son of God, the Great Physician-IATROS, or The Redeemer –GA'AL, LYTRON And even to the Helper; the Holy Spirit. I can call upon the Nature and Characteristics of the Trinity as a whole and the Trinity as three [3] persons in One, individual and personal to me. This is all possible because God meets us right in our need, whatever that need is, He is *ALL* things to ALL of His children.

To understand what I want to share next it will be necessary to 'call upon' The Alpha and the Omega – ALPHA KAI OMEGA, as Jesus reveals Himself in the book of Revelation; "I am the Alpha and the Omega, the First and the Last, the Beginning and the End." Revelation 22:13 Three times He states His name, and each time He makes it more plain to see Who He is, within time itself and in relation to people in general. Alpha meaning *First* and Omega meaning *Last*. He is the First and the Last. He should be the First thing you think of upon waking each morning and the Last thing you think upon before resting at night. He is First, as in the First Born of many Brethren and He is Last to speak in the last book of the Bible, giving Him the Last and Final Word. Jesus is the Beginning and the End. Present at the beginning of time and creation of earth and All the inhabitants thereof, He is with us to the End of Days. Here is what I want you to see, Jesus is able to move from the Beginning of time to the End of time. All things are revealed to Him.

He already knows the outcome of every situation. When Jesus gives John the revelations found in the book with that title, he is showing John what is to come. How can He do that unless He has already seen it for Himself? This book was written long ago, before you or I were ever living and breathing, but not before we were known. He always knew you would be here, today and for such a time as this. There was no accident and there was no mistake. That is an argument we shall save for another day. For now the key to understand; Jesus is the One who is and who was, and the One who is to come. Present, past and Future, All in ALL, for ALL times.

Long ago, I realized that if I was going to believe even one word of the bible, then I had to believe it all, each and every word, especially the difficult words because difficult words are the ones that fight the flesh which breeds the doubt, until you allow Jesus' life giving words [LOGOS] to sink in and make the necessary changes within your core.

"Teaching them to observe all that I commanded you; and lo, I am with you always, even to the end of the age." –Matthew 28:20

When we come to Christ, as in our conversion or Salvation story, we are immediately transferred over from the kingdom of darkness into marvelous light. Take note here-that means your identity was located in darkness and you became light, through Jesus and His victory on the Cross. This is the only way to gain access. Through the Blood of the Lamb. Once Salvation comes to your soul, your identity changes. Here is where it can seem tricky, even though it is not if you let it sink in. You are from God (your soul), born (flesh realm) into a sinful world (satan's arena), but then given a choice to return to God (your soul), leaving your flesh here on earth to rot and return to the dirt from which it was derived.

The journey of this soul is called your life. The devil wants to steal your life away, keeping you in darkness with him by any means necessary. He will steal, kill and destroy to keep your soul away from God. His favorite weapon is to lie to you and make you think things are better or worse than you understand them to be. I believe that this is what happened to my son, and to his father as well. They were the 5th and 6th ones to die by suicide in a 40 year span of the father's side of the family. One didn't know who he was in Christ, the other had forgotten along the path. I truly understand that it can be difficult at times to believe you belong to God, this is part of each person's life goal, to answer this question within their own heart and lives.

Sometimes in prayer ministry I am asked questions that weigh heavy on a person's heart. They have faith; I know this because they actually came to prayer ministry, but there are doubts which swirl around and poke at them, causing their belief to be shaken. It was a series of these questions, mingled with some of my own that I 'settled' for myself in earlier years, before the prayer ministry became a regular part of my life, these questions may even be familiar to you, as I have found "nothing is new under the sun."

Q. "Why do bad things happen today if God loves His children?"
A. Unequivocally I respond; there is nothing no - thing   bad in God. He is eternally good and good eternally! Every good and perfect gift is from the Father of Lights. There is not a counter punch for that in the Bible. I know, I have looked.

As this piece of writing is going into publication, I have some personal anniversaries in the not too distant future. My beautiful son

Justin took his own life at the age of 22. He was so amazing, and never saw that in himself. There are no words for this kind of ache. He followed in his father's path.

His sister, nearly lost the battle as well, at the tender age of 8 she put a rope around her neck and jumped off the swing set. Who does that? Someone who hears the whisper of the spirit of death and thinks it is her friend, because it has always been around and "talking" to her. What we don't know can hurt us, possibly even kill us. I myself bear the scars of a failed attempt at the age of 16.

Yes, I believe we can be stalked by what we do not understand. I am grateful every day that I "failed" it was my greatest triumph to "live". -And now live only for Jesus. My daughter is alive and successfully making her way across the canvas of her life. We will never rest until the Truth of God and the Power of His love are shared with all that we can reach. I stopped asking why? And started looking into how? When?

Finding the Beginning by Going to the End

Of course we consider [suicide] a bad thing. Anyone who was ever left behind after a loved one took their own life knows just how bad it can get. Let's turn this a bit and look at it from another angle. Suicide; from the angle of Spiritual Warfare - I know it's difficult to be objective here, but necessary or I wouldn't ask you to do it. Right from the beginning of the Good Book you can see a pattern developing, between God's people and the enemy of their soul. It is no wonder that satan would desire for us to be dead, it is the only way to halt the power of God's chosen. You know the story of Adam & Eve and the serpent. Serpent, as in a snake. That's a snake, and even the biggest snake is still a snake.

Yet, consider this in Revelations it shows a dragon [enraged] still known as satan.

Q. How does a snake become a dragon?

V.3 "Then I witnessed in heaven another significant event. I saw a large red dragon with seven heads and ten horns, with seven crowns on his heads."

[Note: Large Red Dragon]

V.7 "Then there was war in heaven. Michael and his angels fought against the dragon and his angels."

[Note: the angels fought the dragon]

V.8 "And the dragon lost the battle, and he and his angels were forced out of heaven."

[Note: the dragon lost]   **Hallelujah!**

V.9 "This great dragon—the ancient serpent called the devil, or Satan, the one deceiving the whole world—was thrown down to the earth with all his angels."

[Note: the ancient serpent called the devil or Satan; he started out as a snake. Well, actually he was a beautiful angel and covered in precious stones until his pride got too big, then the fighting began. He was a sneaky snake up in Heaven even before he became known as the serpent in the Garden of Eden.] God always reveals our true nature.

V.10 "Then I heard a loud voice shouting across the heavens, "It has come at last—salvation and power and the Kingdom of our God and the authority of his Christ.
For the accuser of our brothers and sisters
has been thrown down to earth—
the one who accuses them before our God day and night."

[Note: v.10a this all refers to Jesus and to His anointing. The brothers and sisters are you and I and all that have come to Jesus.]

[Note: v.10b the enemy still accusing us day and night.
If you have ever accused yourself of wrong and you keep at it day and night heaping condemnation upon yourself, who do you think you would be acting like? Just something to think about.]

V.11 "And they have defeated him by the blood of the Lamb
and by their testimony.
And they did not love their lives so much
that they were afraid to die."

[Note: V. 11 ...by their testimony....
This is OUR testimony of Jesus in our lives. This testimony is so powerful that it brings defeat to the devil, so if satan can squelch that testimony and shut you up he will try his best to do so.
It's really all he's got.]

As we continue on with this portion of scripture, I would like to encourage you that if you are strong in these areas, it is helpful to find others that you can come along side of. God may place people in your life who do not know these things, but need to. If you have identified any lies about your identity, it is always beneficial to fast and pray. You are beloved and you are here on earth for a divine purpose. There are no mistakes in God's perfect plan.

You are part of that plan.

May the Lord bless you and keep you as you find freedom in Jesus Christ of Nazareth.

Praying all things In His Name.

A War for Our Souls

Authority. There is a whole bunch happening here, all at once. It is a Holy war for our very souls. In the last chapter, I wanted you to see the contrast of good and evil. To see that because God has created you to be in His image, that you would become washed clean when you came into a Salvation experience with Jesus. That all the T's were crossed and all the I's dotted. I wish it went that smoothly.

You become a new creation, that fact can't be disputed. However, to assume that it's over and you just sip ice tea from here on out. Well.... Your soul has been snatched away from the flames that much is true. But the real work begins in dealing with your soul's wounds. Jesus is perfect, the people He saves are not. We celebrate your eternal entry into Heaven, you have made the best choice! What do you do now? What if your problems don't disappear overnight? What if they get worse, before they get better?

Let's finish the portion of scripture where we left off in Revelations.

V. 12 "Therefore, rejoice, O heavens! And you who live in the heavens, rejoice!
But terror will come on the earth and the sea, for the devil has come down to you in great anger, knowing that he has little time."

[Note: V. 12 But terror will come on earth.... For the devil has come down.
1. First of all I want to point out that the devil [Lucifer] HAD to be cast out of Heaven because he was so unholy that he could not remain.
2. Second you see he came down (to us) in great anger.
   He was bent on revenge, and now his anger is pointed at us.]

V.13 "When the dragon realized that he had been thrown down to the earth, he pursued the woman that had given birth to the male child."

[Note: V. 13 When the dragon realized; by the time he knew what was happening it was too late. That means in an instant he was thrown down, Jesus says He seen him "Fall like lightning." The devil is angry and pursues the woman who gave birth to the male child (Jesus)]

Jump to Verse 17

V. 17 "And the dragon was angry at the woman and declared war against the rest of her children—all who keep God's commandments and maintain their testimony for Jesus."

[Note: V. 17 .....Against the rest of her children. You might ask who is this woman?

Every person on earth except Adam and Eve were born from a female.

This I believe is in reference to the virgin birth of Jesus, conceived by the Holy Spirit over shadowing Mary. The same "type" of experience is ours as we are "birthed" into our own Salvation for all eternity with Jesus. That too takes place by the Holy Spirit being the 'vehicle', or the elevator as I explain it to my kids. Holy Spirit is our connection in the spirit realms, Jesus is our bridge to Father God.]

Remember that the devil was already engaged in a war, while he was in Heaven...

So now the devil wants to keep the same war going and it is against us...God's children.

Well, that's enough for anyone to be scared straight! Unless, you know how the story turns out.

Even after all that, I still made another discovery. Revelations goes on to reveal even more shocking news. And even more questions arise.

Q. Satan gets his power from something or someone?

Q. What can his source be?

Keep in mind that everything the devil does is a counterfeit of what Jesus did and does. Only you can count on it being twisted and bent towards evil. Scripture shows that we [God's children] obtain all power and authority from Jesus (Luke 9:1) in

Q. So by whom does he get this power?

Satan [the ancient serpent] actually derives his power from people. The nerve of that beast! "How can that be true?" I am glad you asked.

Let's move to the next set of scriptures, before wrapping this up.

Revelations 13:1 "Then I stood on the sand of the sea. And I saw a beast rising up out of the sea." KJV

Revelations 13:2 "having seven heads and ten horns, and upon his horns ten crowns, and upon his heads the name of blasphemy." KJV

[Note: Beast rises out of the sea, from V. 13 to V.17 the dragon is persecuting the woman, and trying to drown her with a flood of water, which comes from the mouth of the dragon. Hold that thought.]

Now jump to Revelations 17:13 (to me, this is some of the most disturbing scripture I have ever read)

V.13 "These are of one mind, and they will give their power and authority to the beast. V. 14 They will make war on the Lamb, and the Lamb will overcome them, for He is Lord of lords and King of kings, and those who are with him are called, chosen, and faithful."

V. 15 Then he said to me, "The waters which you saw, where the harlot sits, are peoples and multitudes, nations and tongues."

Here is what just happened, after the dragon made the flood with his mouth, the beast rose up out of that water. A reflection of the dragon. Just as we are to be a reflection of Jesus, the devil has a reflection also.

The flood from the dragon's mouth was blasphemies against the

Holy God and His tabernacle and Heaven. In others words, he is lying. Revelations 13:3 states that the world marveled and followed the beast. This is regular people of the world speaking and living against God. A flood of them, and the beast gains power from them because they are of one mind and they are choosing to give away their power!

What I hope you have seen in all this, is to realize that when you don't know your authority, you get beat up pretty badly, you are tricked and much is stolen from you along the way. You are told that the Holy Spirit doesn't work in us today, or that He doesn't give gifts, it was all for the book of Acts. Even that the Old Testament isn't relevant anymore. All lies, spoken from a position of not knowing who Jesus is. The Bible does say that the gifts of God are irrevocable, Jesus Himself quotes the OT and He wouldn't do that if there were no relevance. Miracles still take place today. I have witnessed more than I can number. The flood speaks against the Holy God, we cannot allow ourselves to look nor speak like the beast.
We have authority to rise up against that dragon.

It comes full circle though, because how would you know your authority in Christ if you have not yet learned your identity in Christ Jesus?
I could go on in length and list off all the ways that you have authority, I could also just give you a copy of an altar training manual that I wrote, which served to train and equip those coming into inner healing ministry and who would find their place at the altar of God each Sunday to wage war against the devil. Taking back what was stolen. I am not going to do that here.

The irony of this war is that it is not fought with angry words nor swords that pierce the flesh, coming at us as judgement bent on demanding change. Rather, this is a war fought in the most unlikely way, fought with dose after dose of love for one another. To show by example that the goodness of God is in fact amongst the land of the living, and by this goodness another believer is led (not pushed) to repentance. It is a work of the Holy Spirit, one of conviction to be who we were always meant to be, a child of God. Not forced to accept our flaws spoken with the sting of condemnation and judgement where fear rules the day.

We have authority only by our position in Jesus. We didn't earn it, and it must never be squandered on those who do not desire to have the Prince of Peace in their own lives. Not all will be vessels of honor, let the Spirit decide. Trust in the Lord to do the real ministering, offer what you have that no devil can take. Your human touch, the way you can smile at another, the way you can sit with a grieving person even if you do not know what to say, you are there and you show that someone does care.

You minister love where the world would throw stones, you be to another, what you wanted for yourself and did not get. A friend, a good listener. A trusted confidant that would never gossip. Be an intercessor, praying for others needs and hurts. In these things you will find your authority is rooted in love.

> *"For whatever is **born of God** conquers the world;"*
> *-1 John 5:4 (emphasis added)*

Victory at The Cross

Responsibility. What does responsibility mean to the Christian, who walks by faith? This is a very individual area, unique even as the call on our lives. For some it means the mission field, for another it could be to pastor a church. The equipping of the saints for the work of the ministry. Our reasonable service. The commitment to the process of change during the seasons of growth. A determined purpose to know Christ. Lifelong goals. Life changing destinies! Because you remained when so many times it seemed easier to turn and walk away. You loved Him because He first loved you.

Some truths are far more penetrating than the lies which fly as endless arrows, banging up your armor.

This is the most precious of levels or stages to me. After some time has passed and you begin to realize that you can live above the snake line, you slow a little. You rest more and worry less. You take time to soak in the River of Life and you just enjoy being. It's okay to stop and listen to the wind in the trees and to feel the life in the universe all around you. You are maturing In Christ, I did not say that you have arrived, but you have learned volumes. When someone quotes scriptures like Isaiah, "In quietness and in confidence shall be your strength." You just smile and reflect, yes He has taught you much and now out of love, you have an overwhelming desire to share His love with others. Your responsibility compels you to this lifestyle. Where else would we go?

"Then judgement shall dwell in the wilderness and righteousness remain in the fruitful field, and the work of righteousness shall be peace, and the effect of righteousness, quietness and assurance forever. And my people shall dwell in a peaceable habitation. And in sure dwellings and in quiet resting places."
–Isaiah 32:16-18

In the end, even death is a lie.

"The testimony of Jesus Christ is the spirit of prophecy."

Wrapping It All Up

As you can now see, there was a multitude of foul play. Thousands of years of the devil perfecting his schemes.

My truth is this, God doesn't desire anything bad for His children, He only has good to give away.

You can find the answer located in the first book of the bible. In Genesis we can read that Adam & Eve came up against the same thing as the one who abused me as a child. Temptation to do evil, to go against the perfect will of God. This choice has been made time and again down through the ages. We call it sin, and not too many would say it doesn't exist.

Every person alive has a few things in common right from the start of their lives. God gives us free will, and that allows us the choice to choose Him. That is the original function of this option. People use it to also choose the other side of the coin. We can boil it down to this, if you have had evil done to you or you have given away less than your best, it was a free will choice and Father God never intended for you to use this gift of free will in a negative way. But it happens and that person in your life that hurt you or hurt someone close to you, they made that choice and took the choice for good and handed it over to evil. The devil only has a place if we give him a place.

When your life ends and you make it to Heaven you will not stand before the Lord of Glory to answer for what others did to you, but you will answer for the way you chose to respond to your offense. This is the only real choice you have left to make if you find yourself in a rough patch.

Some words of encouragement:
- God sees it all. The good you do, the injustices done to you, the ways you try and even the retaliation that might be in your heart towards another that has done wrong.
- He sees it all. Somehow He works it all too good, for those who love Him and are called according to His purposes. You are not alone in any of this.

We all become EQUAL at the CROSS.

"Therefore, since God in his mercy has given us this new way, we never give up." ~2 Corinthians 4:1

"Everyone who calls on the name of the Lord will be saved." ~Romans 10:13

To sum it all up I would make this statement.
- WE are the ones who empower the devil, beyond his own rebellion. (*OUCH*) He doesn't always *take* from us, sometimes we just let him have it.

Man believes lies and lives life out of lies.

Suicide is the granddaddy of all lies. This is a focus that I have dug very deeply into. Once the lies are exposed, we can begin to firmly grasp the Truth, which is the love of God and replace what was once a lie with the new perspective and then the life of victory will unfold before you.

I have so much more to share, we are just getting started really.

Prayer Portions

In the next part entitled our wounded SOUL, I will open up about my first run in with suicide. Remember, people have limits of how much they can take in all at once. I will not overwhelm you with more than you can process in one session.

Because this is such a serious subject, I would like to ask you to consider taking a brief moment to pray and perhaps listen to some soaking worship music. Any anointed music will work for this, the purpose of the exercise is to be still and to wait upon the Lord.

I recommend Grace Williams; Fire Fall. (Album) *Spirit Come* (song) I'm sure you could find it on Youtube.com

As you "soak" just allow the music to carry you where the Lord *Wills* for you to go. If you read something in this text that has stirred you, please don't resist it.

Journal anything that comes up, you will be able to utilize it in the next chapter.

This is your time now, to draw close to God and feel the love He wants to pour over you. Fear not, for surely the Kingdom will come close to you in your obedience and humility.

Need a jumpstart in prayer? Try these

Do not give the devil a place

> -Ephesians 4:27 and do not give the devil a foothold.
> [Berean Study Bible]

And do not give the devil an opportunity to work.[ISV]
Do not give the devil your power.

"Ye are of God, little children, and have overcome them: because greater is he that is in you, than he that is in the world." 1 John 4:4 [KJV]

Say this to yourself: ...Greater is He that is in me, than he that is in the world. {Just how many times should you say it? Until you believe it!}

"Blessed are the peacemakers: for they shall be called the children of God." Matthew 5:9 [KJV]

-No, in all these things we are more than conquerors through him who loved us. For I am sure that neither death nor life, nor angels nor rulers, nor things present nor things to come, nor powers, nor height nor depth, nor anything else in all creation, will be able to separate us from the love of God in Christ Jesus our Lord. Romans 8:37-39

But you, O Lord, are a God merciful and gracious, slow to anger and abounding in steadfast love and faithfulness. -Psalm 86:15

CHAPTER TWO

Our Wounded SOUL

Leaving Normal

Should such a place exist; normal is not where I reside. I thought I wanted my life to be regular or "normal".

I want to consider myself to be just a regular person, for all that I have lived or done, I would conclude that in many ways I am like everyone else. To wish for a healthy family, a nice home or peace in the world. I do not feel like I am so different nor am I special or more important than others. Especially to God, He loves us all.

Death has a way of altering a person. I'm going to make a bold statement and say that Suicide is worse than death. Suicide and the aftermath leave you with holes all over your heart and soul. Try as you might to pick up the pieces and reconstruct yourself, you are left holding a mess.

The new reality for a survivor of suicide is devastating, the questions, the guilt, the longing to see your loved one again. If others around us would just accept that we can't go back to the way we were before, even if we wanted to, there is no way because we are permanently and forever changed.

After my son took his life, I changed again, I could feel it inside as I wrestled with all the emotions. Some I knew were really "bad" they wanted to take up residency within my heart. Such things like bitterness and anger. These things made me terribly uncomfortable and I wanted no part of a life filled with more turmoil. As I noticed deep down within myself that other feelings and emotions were fighting for center stage, I began to give into them.

Maybe if I were searching for things that stand out in myself during a moment of introspect, I might notice a hunger inside. You could almost call it ravenous because it never seems to be satisfied, and that hunger, this insatiable appetite is to know the Lord. It is what drives me and pushes me forward. I would say that by now, I do not know what it is to live without this craving. If it were to leave me, I have no doubt that this hunger would be replaced with something else, but it wouldn't be holy and it wouldn't be welcomed.

By nature we are all predisposed to have a longing for our Creator. What I am talking about here, goes beyond that, it is more deliberate and not in any way hidden from me, waiting to be discovered. It is like a living, breathing- *person.*

Over time though you just start to notice things, the kind of things that keep reoccurring and there seems to be no explanation for it, other than it's different. It can be unsettling at first, to discover that the thing which is different, is you. That is to say, maybe what was thought of to be 'normal' like everyone else, really is not standard issue after all.

There is a force within our universe that is stronger than death, or its evil twin Suicide.

This realization, and more to the point, a REVELATION of Jesus Christ has a way of changing an individual. So, you're going along in life and you are so intertwined with the workings and character of Who Jesus is, that you don't even realize the amazing changes that have taken place! My books are all about the changes I am aware of, the ones that I saw happen and stood breathless to behold.

Along the way though, in capturing so much of it in one place, I must step back and marvel at the way Jesus has revealed Himself, yet again in putting all of this down into one account; a three part series, none-the-less. You see, what I am trying to say is that, where I saw nothing special, where I couldn't "find value", Jesus did find those things, and of all places, right in the midst of my stormy life. What I could look at and say "There is nothing here to work with." Jesus can just smile that smile, which says "I know, more about this than you do, rest in me, I got this." I hope that you have seen, or felt the Lord smile at you in such a way. It's like a warm, safe hug that melts you from the inside out. What a place to dwell in...

This is when I knew that things were going to get better and that I wasn't stuck in the bone -depth pain for the rest of my time on earth.

Sure, "normal" and I parted ways a long time ago. Upon leaving, I entered into another place, a parallel universe which stopped time and moved back and forth across generations. I had gained access to the secret places with God and He didn't mind my being there, I even think that He waited for me to find Him and to hang out a while.

James, a servant of God and of the Lord Jesus Christ, To the twelve tribes in the Dispersion: Greetings. Consider it pure joy, my brothers, when you encounter trials of many kinds, because you know that the testing of your faith develops perseverance...
~James 1:2-3

Through these tough times. He points out that there is a meaning and a tangible value to getting through tough patches and the most important part, I have found, is HOW you get through.

In this chapter I want to share with you a behind the scenes look at the ways your soul (your inner man) gets hurt and how it could be through events that span your entire life.

To do this, I will have to share what took place in my own life and just how the Lord had to re-build my foundation, as He re-built me. For I was, more than once, completely smashed to pieces.

As I open up, and just become transparent in this amazing walk I am on with Jesus, I pray you can be open to what I mean by no longer being normal.

It is here that healing flows and love reigns.

Where I can finally say, "It is well with my soul."
So it can be found (my answer) in Romans and 2Corinthians; faith to faith and Glory to Glory. It's my faith and His Glory.

My Darkest Hour

All of my drinking began when I was a young girl, about the age of 5, this was the time of life where I tried cigarettes too. That didn't last long though because my dad decided to make my older sister and I eat those cigarettes, and let me tell you that is a moment which nobody forgets. We were so sick and I think we may actually have turned green. I never smoked, I don't know if my sister did. We were not close growing up.

My parents owned a bar and they pretty much left us to roam freely about, I was around 9 years old. We loved it, we were wild. My little brother and I were very close, we did everything together. We swam in the lakes that were near the bar and we got into a bunch of near death scrapes. When I look back on all the things we did, I can't believe we weren't kidnapped or taken away from my parents. One of the things we did while unsupervised was to drink the left over alcohol from the parties. This went on for years. By the time I was 21 I didn't even drink anymore, I was so tired of feeling hungover. When my first husband and I lived in Chicago he took me to a restaurant in a high rise tower for my 21st birthday. I did not order any alcohol. I did however just about faint from embarrassment when the whole place started singing Happy Birthday! Being the center of attention was never my thing.

Now, I am getting ahead of myself. The teenage years must be addressed for you to really have the big picture of just how chaotic my life was.

I entered foster care when I was 13. There is a whole list of things that went wrong. It won't enrich your life any to know the details, let's just say that when I went through prayer counseling to begin Inner Healing; my prayer counselor had to go into counseling. She told me afterwards that she had to pray to forgive my dad. It was so long ago and I have forgiven my dad too. It took some time because I was really stubborn and felt justified in my hatred. I suffered from PTSD and I had formed multiple personalities to find a way to cope with my pain and the distortion of what I believed was possible but could not attain it in real time.

I wanted to get free of the torment of others and I searched for that freedom and love, only to be continually disappointed and left with another truckload of rejection. Each time I moved to a new group home or foster home it would start again. Each time my own family rejected me instead of embracing me with love, I turned my anger, pain and hatred against myself, internalizing and keeping what happened to me stirred up. I didn't know that forgiving them would release me from my prison. I carried this baggage around for years, and I was losing hope of any change for the better.

All of those years led up to me having the encounter with suicide that I am about to share. It wasn't any one thing that pushed me over, it was a combination of years and years of the same type of thing happening. Like a battering ram from hell, hit after hit. How could I stop this onslaught against me?

As far as I know this was my first encounter with the spirit of death. I have come to understand that this spirit was literally stalking me over my entire lifetime. Right from the beginning in the womb. Rejection was present from both of my parents, and my paternal grandparents. Stories were told to me as I grew up, confirmed by actions of the adults in my life. When I got older, in my 40's my older sister (51 weeks older, exactly) told me stories too, and we were able to collaborate a timetable and verify events that took place, which I guess we started to tell ourselves we made those things up in our heads. To my dismay, they were true. Things like being left unattended in an upstairs room with only a light on and a handful of stuffed toys to keep me company. We looked through random pictures and both came up with the same house and same memory of that room upstairs with the slanted wall that had a cut out in it. Having to crawl in and the door closing behind.

I never wanted to go past the string that hung down from the light bulb, it was dark back in there and I cried for someone, anyone to talk to me. The pictures confirmed that we were both under 5 years old when we lived in that house.

The avocado green chair that I had to sit in for hours, it spun around and I would spin it until it fell off onto the floor. Even though I got yelled at for doing this, it made the adults come in the room, and they would yank me around and get the chair fixed but they remembered I was there, and that was all I wanted. Negative attention is still attention.

My sister and I both remembered the basements, and the rooms that were down in those cold Michigan cellars. I often wondered why I never saw my sister very much when growing up. I was struck with horror the day she revealed to me which room she was kept in. I only thought the room at the bottom of the stairs was used. There was another to the left and back in the dark corner.

Dear God, the memories that were blocked from coming to the surface could only be worse. I don't want to know and I have left those forgotten memories alone, prayed for them to heal and be covered with the Blood of Jesus. I pray for you too, if you have forgotten years, like I did as a protective measure for your own sanity. I pray that you can be strong enough to handle what is revealed and to rise up above it, for surely you can overcome when you have the Redeemer fighting with you.

In the first part of this book, I shared what happened with my first husband David. He was my high school sweetheart and all that goes with it. I knew him for 16 years, married for 10 of that, when he ended his life at the age of 34. That was my second encounter with suicide. When I think back to how I handled certain parts of my life, and the decisions I made, it is clear that I thought more with my heart than I did with my head. I really believed that David's family was "normal" per say and that they were the perfect example of how a family should act. To this day, I still mimic some of their family behaviors, such as everyone coming to the dinner table and playing board games or gathering on the couch for a movie. I'm sure lots of families do these things, but they were not a part of my household growing up and his family was my introduction to this style of living.

At our house we ate in separate rooms, or not at all sometimes. We didn't play games and were not invited into the room with the TV. We simply stayed outside, all day and all night. We stayed away from the conflict that surely awaited our return. My brother and I used to have little "safe places" that we would go hide in, basically they were deep holes in the ground, dug out to fit two or three people. Scraps of ply-wood were used as the makeshift roof and then covered up with dirt, so as not to be discovered. Our dad never found us in these places. It was the best we could come up with at ages of 8 & 6. The hole-digging went on for many years, whenever we moved my brother and I would construct a new set of hiding places. Going into foster care was what ended the hiding for me.

In the foster homes /group homes I found a new set of challenges and many life situations that I never dreamed of. Some of those were very difficult yet, even now knowing what would take place I still would not have gone back to the home that I left.

What I wouldn't miss was being picked up by my throat, lifted eye level to be yelled at and then tossed to the floor like a Rag doll. I never liked my dad's form of "conditioning" and the way he would have us repeat negative things about ourselves. If you didn't like it you would suffer the fury which followed and that could be a beating or thrown down the stairs or even being made to eat off the floor as he held your face down. These were the easier days. You learned at a young age how to toughen up, take a punch and never, ever let him see your weakness.

When my mother died, he told me that she never loved me. Specifically in a phone conversation he said "I'm 57 years old, and I don't want to be bothered with you, don't call me anymore and you know your mother, she never liked you anyway." It was absurd and I knew he was wrong. You see, I had a secret relationship with my mom. After my little sister was born we would meet up at the grocery store. I could see my baby sister and hold her without fear of my dad. I have many pictures of the first four years in her life and she is sitting inside a grocery cart!

My sweet little sister turned five years old just 4 days after my mother died on her own 49th birthday. I was terrified for her, growing up in a house without my mother's shielding. She had my dad's mother living with them also, but it couldn't have been good because she told me that "Granny tried to drown her once in the toilet."

Through the years, I kept in touch with my little sister as much as I could while she was growing up. As a woman now, with 2 of her own children she refers to me as her mom. That is how her little ones see me, I've become the replacement for the mama she never knew. I've been told by 2 of my 3 siblings that I am the most like my mother, in gentleness, kindness and also in my artistic /creative abilities. I think that is the nicest compliment I could receive and a testimony to how much the Lord brought me through to get me where I am today. The Lord Jesus is faithful to cleanse us from all unrighteousness.

For every incident that I have shared in this story, I kept back 3 or 4 more. I didn't want to cover you in my old "grime". Transparency, requires a boldness to let the truth be known, at a risk of being judged.

I have spent the latter part of my life recovering from my childhood and I have no doubt that if I had not found and pursued the Lord, I would not have made it as far as I have. Or worse, I would have turned out like my earthly father. What a miserable old man he was, and when he died several years after my mother, in a hospital bed, he was alone. Not one of his four children came to say goodbye.

It was the love of the Lord who showed me my dad's heart and that the things he reflected were the only things he had to give. My dad didn't give away love because he didn't possess it in his heart. His short comings didn't have to be mine. I didn't have to become like him. Jesus says this, "If you've seen Me, then you've seen the Father." I was in desperate need of a new Father figure!

It has been a journey of forgiving that man, each time the Lord brings something to my mind which took place, I pray the Blood of Jesus over it, I return to him (my dad) what was his and I take back what was mine, washed and sanctified through the Holy Blood. I forgive him and I leave it at the cross. When I see (recognize) an open door, I first identify the source (hatred, word curse etc.) then I close that door and I break off its connection to my life and to the lives of my children. Doing this stops the enemy from continuing on down through my bloodline. The result of this deliberate effort is to halt, or bind the devil from coming into my life on a technicality, because my blood is now cleansed. My mind and heart should then follow suit.

The benchmark of the revelation in the "Beautiful Light" which Jesus showed me is crucial to my new belief in who I am *IN* Christ.

Self-condemnation has no victory in it.

Well, you can get the general idea that things were less than ideal while I was growing up. Foster care was probably inevitable. My grades never suffered enough for the school to get involved with my parents.

I began fighting a lot and that brought attention to me, it was necessary though because I had reached a point in my life where I could not take any more bullying. My father was a tyrant and for all that I didn't like being in those rooms, I would venture to guess that my mother was trying to protect me from him. He was the reason I left, and my mother was the reason I did not allow myself to be adopted. It was offered to me by a wonderful couple that for the life of me I could not figure out why they were so kind and accepting of my messed up existence. When I told my mother that I was offered this opportunity to be adopted, she asked me not to and I could see how much this whole thing hurt her. I chose not to go through with it, yet I remained close to the foster family for over 30 years now. My mother died 7 years later, on her 49th birthday due to stomach cancer. I was 22 at that time. I remember calling her and she said the most peculiar thing to me

"I was waiting for you to call."

It really struck me hard because two hours after we hung up, she passed from this world to the next. How do you put off death and wait on a phone call? She was a strong woman, although gentle and much too kind for the man who married her.

It was during this time period of foster homes / group homes, constant changes of living arrangements and 5 changes in high schools that I took a glass bottle of mountain dew, broke the end off and dug it into both of my wrists. I had reached my limit. I was so hurt and betrayed and just lost completely at the age of 16. I remember that I had been drinking, and that I found out David was with another girl from school. It was too much for me to deal with. That's no excuse, there is never an excuse good enough for a suicide attempt, but I tried anyway. I was so sure that nobody would even care if I was dead and probably my body would just rot where I dropped. I felt so unloved and truly I didn't even love myself anymore, which had been my heart's condition for many, many years.

I was so angry at myself when I woke up to find that I was still alive, my wrists were bandaged and my life would continue.

"You couldn't even do that right!" I remember telling myself, hearing that negative voice of destruction. It would take years of training myself to speak positively with words of affirmation and love to *me*.

I would like to say that now, I am grateful to the two girls who must have seen what I did and they took me to one of their houses to stop my bleeding. To Kim & Carla I am forever grateful that I did not die that evening and that I lived to have my children and find Salvation through Jesus Christ. If you're reading this, please know I pray for your good fortune and favor of the Lord to bless your lives 100 fold.

To the credit and stability of my foster parents I know that they gave me every effort they could to help my life be better than when I arrived at their home just before turning 14 years old. No matter how many times I was removed by the courts, this family still remained dedicated to my safe keeping and to my returning back into their home. To this day, my purple room is still there in that house. As I watched my foster mom deal with people and work out problems it occurred to me that I could take from others actions what I saw to be good and these traits could become my own.

I wanted to be better than what I was and to change the course of my future from death to a life of abundance, even if I didn't yet know how to put that into words or action.

Somehow, I did graduate from High School on schedule. More credit to my foster mom Linda, she knew I needed that diploma if I was going to begin building a different life. School was never the hard part, grades came easy when I bothered to read the materials. I spent way too much time skipping school and hiding in the library, of all places. I would get detention just so I wouldn't have to go back home, or so I could buy myself time to go do other things before heading back to the foster homes, where I will still to this day be working off my grounding for various times that I skipped school.

Vicious cycles were a regular thing with me.

A girl from the high school asked me once, did I think that if my family had been a better one, would I have stayed with David? I didn't see the pattern then of the abusive father leading into the relationship with the abusive husband. It doesn't always have to be that way, but in my case what I thought was better, was really only a different form. Trading one toxic relationship for another one.

One of my more deeply rooted issues was a broken trust with authority. I couldn't believe that anyone was trust worthy nor would they really try to help a girl like me, one who's own parents didn't even care about her. To say that I had a wounded soul, might come across as an understatement. I was inconsolable and squashed emotionally. Self-esteem, gone. Self-worth, flushed down the toilet with my bulimia issues.

I was dying inside a little bit every day with my own self-hatred eating away at my heart and soul.

Until I met Jesus, I put all my needs upon David. He was there for all of the good and bad of my life from the age of 14 until I turned 30, when he passed. We were two insecure and confused people that didn't trust anyone. But we got married anyway and I thought that was some kind of solution. How many thousands of couples do the same thing to each other every year? I just wanted a family, a normal life and my own place in the world where I could be left alone without ridicule or violent behavior on a daily basis. We began by running away from a small town to a big city. Seems reasonable right?

Here's the thing about being wounded in your inner being-

You don't stop being wounded just because you run from your problems.

I needed an overhaul, a remaking of the devastation to my life. But how, and by what means could this happen?

Now, the journey for you might just be starting, but I pray you will allow it to take place in your life. Nobody ever regrets the first steps of believing they can be better tomorrow, than they were today.

If you identified any "doors" or negative entry points from your own life write them down and take them into prayer, just as I have shown you to do.

Scars of Pain

-j.   5-24-2014 one of the first scriptures that I ever memorized was this: "The Lord is my helper; I will not be afraid. What can man do to me?"

It was a scripture about fear and those first steps in trusting God, Learning to <u>Believe</u> what those words said and allowing them to become life to my dry and thirsty soul. I found so much comfort in the realization [revelation] that God was on my side <u>and</u> He was fighting for me! I was not alone for all the years that I felt like I was.

I had this new truth and if I were brave enough I could begin exploring what it would mean.

I will never forget the night in Bible study when we were gathered around a table in the basement of a tiny church, and a man named Lyle asked us to share our favorite scripture. His face said it all, and I guess I felt kind of dumb for saying that particular scripture. I didn't know very many yet, but I was tired of being afraid and this is what gave me comfort. Let me encourage you now to memorize what gives you strength, it doesn't matter if the person next to you likes a different set of scriptures or no scriptures at all. This is your life and it is your victory that you are going after!

There is a place and a time during our walk with Jesus where you find yourself asking the tough questions. The ones that you hope do not get you struck by lightning just for the thought. Of course God doesn't use lightning nor a big rod to bring us into order, He is in fact very loving and extremely patient.

I can chuckle now, at my immature and weak faith but really, sincerely this is nothing to laugh at, because it is real and it is the issue of the heart that the Lord is trying to get us to see for ourselves. If it is in your heart, you will at some point have to deal with it. Well, you will if

you desire any kind of growth. You may not have had the level of ne-
glect that I did in my childhood, but it still hurts to be rejected no
matter what your age is. Even if it doesn't happen until you are an
adult but find you are getting a divorce, then you're going to wrestle
with new levels of rejection and loss.

Maybe, dear one you never had a weak moment and you could always find it easy to believe every good thing about God. I bless that, I
rejoice with you! What a treasure that is! Your testimony will bear
much fruit and probably sooner than you think, I hope you are sharing
your good news everywhere! Please pray for us, pray for the ones who
have had to fight, kick and scratch to be where you are or the ones
who are not quite there yet. We need the prayer covering of all the
saints of God.

Through this process of writing, (and maybe this is how we are
tested to see where we are...) I kept hearing the voice of the Spirit, He
would randomly ask me "What would you do if you weren't afraid?"
    To this my answer came quickly "I'd write and publish what I know
to be true about you."
    Every equation has two sides. My story has the good and the bad of
what took place leading up to and going beyond the Suicides.

Dark questions of the heart do have a source and I want to share
what was revealed to me, it will take this 3 part series to accomplish
my task.

Did you ever wonder why does God let bad things happen? How
can He sit by and watch, as a child is abused? These questions take on
various forms and degrees of disparity. Whatever your question is dear
friend, take a moment to let it out now and to look it in the eye and say
"I do have this hidden in my heart... "
    This is what I have come to understand, to the question "Why does
God let bad things happen?"
    My answer is straightforward. "He doesn't."
    Every good and perfect gift is from the Father of lights. It goes
against the very nature of WHO God is. While on my journey, I began
to unravel difficult truths I had to allow some things be settled once
and for all. I took this position. The bible is the truth, the words in it
are truth. Later I came to understand that Jesus is the WORD and He is

in fact *Alive.* What joy it is to know this. I let it become truth to me, I read it and studied it. For every question that I found an answer, two more questions confounded me. I realized that head knowledge wasn't going to cut it, I needed a personal relationship with Jesus. The time I spent in the Word started to sink into to my brain and to my surprise it began to sink into my heart. With every step I took towards the Lord, He took two towards closing the gap.

If I were to say that the Bible was the truth, then I would have to believe every single word of it and I would have to accept whatever this Word uncovered for me. I wanted that. I was so hopelessly sold on the idea that for years I prayed for God to show me, show me everything! Oh boy, was I surprised to discover how much He wanted to do just that!

I had the same heart ache as you might have now, the one that wants to be treated right, the one that needs love and understanding not judgment and ridicule. Would anyone ever accept me for who I am? Just the way I am? Many more questions surfaced.

By the time I was 30, I was a widow with a 10 year old boy and a 5 year old girl to care for. I was devastated, feeling very alone and vulnerable.

I went back to drinking as a way to disguise my true loathing of myself and to stop the gnawing feelings of guilt and rejection. I wanted to be anybody but who I was. Anybody who didn't have my history, or my current situation of a suicide to figure out.

"Why did all these things happen to me Lord?" It is too much to bear, I would cry and wring my heart out. I could not believe anything positive about myself.

This is what He whispered back to me,

"I was with you during every bit of what you went through, I never wanted these things for you and I am here now."

I love when He shows up and washes me with His peace. There is no condemnation in His voice or negative ideas.

"So, if I can't change it and I cannot go backwards to do it all over again what do I have?" This was the question in my heart, so I asked Him straight up.

"You have the measure of Faith that I have placed within you." I imagine He was smiling when He said that part.

Forward.
The only direction that gave me peace.

I have to go forward, in order to do that I must wade through the muck and the mire to get to the other side. It would take courage, and an investment of time. It would also take a commitment. Alone in my house one day, after getting a DUI, Jesus caught up to me in my kitchen. I would talk to him all the time (even though I was not technically saved) I would run from him too as He pursued me. I was approaching the top of the stairs and I felt his hands rest on my shoulders, like someone would do if they were about to look you in the eye and didn't want you to look away. He had a very sobering set of choices to share with me. Looking me straight in the eye He said "Pay attention, you can have the life that you are building for yourself but it will be very dark and you're children will not be in it. Or you can have a life in the Light with your children." I knew He was done playing my games. I knew Him enough that I also realized deep down inside that He was right and that I better stop my foolishness. I didn't stop yet though. Within six months I had another DUI, since the first one was out of state and probably the only reason I didn't get a felony charge against me. I consider it Mercy from the Lord. I did not like those 9 hours that I spent in the county jail either. The whole thing was so stupid on my part, I only had two beers on tap, and I was less than a mile from my home. I should have walked. I was celebrating that I just bought my house. Nobody cared. What an idiot I was and I kept making a mess of every good thing that was placed in front of me.

My license was taken away and I had finals to go to, so I drove again and got pulled over. I was in a technical institute obtaining my computer science degree, yet I was too nimble headed to see that these two lives were colliding into each other and only one could stay. I chose to leave the darkness and walk towards the Light. Yes, walk because I was now without a means of transportation.

(Did you catch all that negative self-talk?)

I began to allow my conversations with God to carry on, and I even began praying albeit the prayers were more based in my wants and needs then in any Kingdom mindset. I remember telling Him some really specific things about the next husband I wanted, smart with construction and not a stuffy office type, patient and would love the two children I already have, the list went on ...blue eyes and not brown, outdoor type, not a tie wearing know it all but somebody real...

What nerve I had to ask anything of the Lord, yet He wanted me to ask and I think He wanted me to dream *beyond* my problems and my past; to get beyond myself.

I met Michael in the mix of all this trouble I was in and wouldn't you know -right down to the blue eyes! He was stronger than me emotionally and somehow he saw right through my false front that I put up. He wanted to get married, I resisted though for nearly 3 years. I had made a vow to never remarry, but that wasn't the Lord's intention when He brought Michael into my life.

The kids and I began to attend the church that Michael's grandmother went to and AJ (who later became my mentor) it was so filled with life and love. Because of my DUI troubles, I had community service to work off and wouldn't you know, the church had some things that I could do for them. So we cleaned out the horse stables and I typed up the Sunday sermons. Yes, that is the Lord's sense of humor right there, having me focused on the Word of God and learning scripture while I got myself right with Him and with society. That is a heaping dose of Grace and I did not miss the goodness in what He was doing for me, or within me.

It is after all - the goodness of God which leads us to

repentance...

Broken Vessels

Was anyone ever so secure in themselves as our Lord and Saviour Jesus? He is the standard, the only ONE that walked this earth and got it right.

Truth is we are all broken. Not one perfect, yet all are on the road to perfection as we follow the Lord. I believe it comes down to perspective. Are we asking the right questions? Questions of ourselves and of those around us. How can you arrive at your destination, if you have never taken time to decide where it is that you want to go?

Let's start there. What is the goal? Reading a book about soul wounds is not the average nightly reading material, right? There is something else, and we both know it...
Take a minute and think it over, I'll wait...

Did you decide on Freedom? Peace?? Or just some Answers???
Maybe Inner Healing? A deeper relationship with Christ? To stop hating, you and all those around you? To stop crying and falling apart several times a day? To let love win, and begin to feel the effects of forgiveness as it washes you clean, setting you free as well as the offender?

We are all broken. To what degree and to the length of time healing takes place is all up to you, it's in your hands, your control. Truly, you can decide right now, today -that this internal struggle will end. You can turn this ship around! Isn't it great to know that you don't always have to trudge along as you have been?

But, HOW? That is part of the process! You didn't get here in your predicament overnight, so be patient and trust that it is doable and that any effort and every minute invested in yourself is WORTH it, you are worth it. Can you say that? Can *you say* I (_____fill in name) AM WORTH EVERY EFFORT TO SAVE!

If you struggled with that, don't worry it is just the beginning of unraveling the lies and removing the foothold that the deceiver of our souls has offered your mind as a solution. You and I have bought into lies and untruths all of our lives. What is false seems true. That leaves the Truth to seem false. Like the truth that you are the apple of God's eye (personally, I stumbled on that one) I believed that I was too far gone, and beyond repair. I am so grateful that Jesus didn't give up on me even though I was ready to give up on myself.

We are all broken. Accepting that and loving each other in-spite of it, is the love Jesus imparts to us and we are all capable of it. I want to shine a light on a piece of the "path" or journey that I myself went down and help you understand that you can change, you can be better and Jesus died on the cross to bring you back into the fold. To secure your place in eternity with your Creator. You are worth it. You are loved and cherished and wanted!

So, why then do you feel like a wrung out dishrag? A doormat that people wipe their feet on, used and abused. Tossed aside and unappreciated, maybe? Well, you get the point. There is a reason and I want to share what I have found out. What I myself had to come to terms with, if you can be brave and face the truth, it will set you free.

"And whom the Son sets free, is free indeed."

A Witness

Hello, My Name is Patricia...
I'm a world class self-hater, in recovery. A shattered vessel without any glue. Stunned and immobilized by grief; waves upon waves of grief, thick and suffocating.
Multiple suicides left me filled with every ugly emotion. Guilt mixed with shame ruled my day. Everything that had ever gone wrong was my fault, or so I thought. My cross was heavy and much more than I could bear up under. Constantly the lies swirled around my head, growing within my heart. When will it ever end? Is death my only escape too?

Hello, My Name is Patricia...
I'm a daughter of the King. I'm holy and beloved. Set in heavenly places to rule and reign with Christ. I'm redeemed and restored. Set FREE of the curse that threatened my existence. Now clothed in garments of white, I carry a double edged

sword.

One forged in the fires of hell, and blessed by the great I AM.

He has called me, for my very name means Victorious and Overcomer!

I am free to receive love and to give love. Forgiveness is my crown. I fought long and hard to soar with the eagles. I have traded yokes with My Saviour, for He knew I could not find my own way out, so He took it all, every weight and every last bit of baggage that I lugged around from childhood to adulthood.

Jesus dances over me, and I am the apple of His eye!

I will proclaim His wondrous deeds!

You see the difference that being a Witness in Christ has on a person's life? It is an amazing thing to be free of all the old pain that the "old nature" carried around. This is perspective, and I want to show you a few things about a divinely guided perspective. We serve a mighty Creator and He has made all provision for us to live a holy life.

It is our choices that restrict our reach into the holy of holies.

God never falters, He never falls short nor grows weak and weary. He is steadfast and in Him there is no shadow of turning. I can count on Him, to be strong. I can trust in Him to get me to the other side of my troubles.

What does your perspective sound like? Are you unsure of Who it is to which you belong? Do you wonder if your life will ever get better? Do you view the world from a top down mindset, or are you only focused on what you can see in the immediate or what is chasing you from your past?

Can't seem to keep a hold on the peaceful or the calmness that is fleeting? Tired of being angry and hurt all the time, easily offended? Are you ready for a change and a new window to look out of? Hope sounds like this; "There has to be another way, and I'm not going to stop until I find it." Those were my very words, and such was my determination at the age of 13 when I left home in search of a better life.

Only to find a whole mess of new troubles awaited me. Yet, I never let go of believing that there was more, it was out there and I just had to keep searching until I found it. To me, those thoughts are evidence of God's pursuit because He placed that grain of faith within me even before I was saved by grace.

Death passed by me, on many occasions I felt its cold breath and heard its pitiful begging. "Nobody cares, so why continue living?" "Why won't it just leave me alone?" I'd wonder. How could I live, in the shadow that it had cast over my life? Eventually the Truth did break through to my heart removing the shackles and casting light into the darkest areas. I know death has a place but I no longer live in fear of it.

The Spiritual Battle

There is an internal battle going on. **A war raging in the Spirit realms and within our own being.** This war; fought with invisible weapons and manifesting in physical form through sickness and disease in our bodies (the flesh). It is a graphic image to behold, yet the understanding of it is so important. I want you to grasp this, the sheer magnitude of knowing this will change the way you think and most assuredly -how you respond to the spiritual attacks on your life.

"For the weapons of our warfare are not carnal, but mighty through God to the pulling down of strongholds, pulling down imaginations and every high thing that exalts itself against the knowledge of God, and bringing into captivity every thought into the obedience of Christ;" 2Corinthians 10:4-5

There are two parallel worlds that exist and move through time, in synchrony. At exactly the same moment that we are living out our lives right now, there are things taking place in the spiritual realm, but you only catch glimpses of it. Especially if you are gifted as a prophet, or in my instance a Seer. That is how I know it is happening, but it is Biblical too and I will share that real soon.

Let's use a movie example to further illustrate my point. In the Lord of the Rings; Frodo Baggins has a ring that makes him disappear when he puts it on his finger, but he is still present in the moment, he can see those around him but they cannot see him, this gives him information that can be useful later on, in my case that is prayer ministry. Only, I don't have a ring. I have the Holy Spirit.

Another example is similar to being in a room before someone gets there, and when they arrive, they do not see you there. So they come and go without even acknowledging you or expecting you to be present. Later, you are in conversation with them and you reveal a detail from that moment in time (the overlap) and you are correct, but they have no idea how you knew, and you have little to no way of explaining it either.

For me, this is the Revelation from the Holy Spirit. When this happens, it is because the Lord wants to work in that person's life and has been unable to reach them directly. Remember, He can use a donkey to talk to us if He can't find an actual person willing to bring the message. Similar to the fact that the rocks and the trees will cry out in Exaltation if no people will Praise Him. I don't know about you, but I never want to be out done by the leaves!

Biblically we can see many examples of this playing out, spiritual happenings overlapped with natural time frames. Let's look at this piece of scripture from the book of Daniel (Old Testament) chapter 10. The archangel Gabriel comes to Daniel, during his time of fasting...

V.12 Then he continued, "Do not be afraid, Daniel. Since the first day that you set your mind to gain understanding and to humble yourself before your God, your words were heard, and I have come in response to them. V.13 But the prince of the Persian kingdom resisted me twenty-one days. Then Michael, one of the chief princes, came to help me, because I was detained there with the king of Persia. V. 14 Now I have come to explain to you what will happen to your people in the future, for the vision concerns a time yet to come."

Do you see that? Not one, but two archangels were there to fight! This was all taking place in the Spirit Realm, while Daniel lived his life out in the natural. It says that Daniel was standing on the beach of the Tigris River. Praying. I believe that Daniel's prayers gave strength and added fortitude to the battle in favor of the angels. Yes, the prayers of the righteous man availeth much. You can listen to the teaching I did on Daniel and his prayer if you go to my YouTube channel.

Another amazing example is from John in the book of Revelations (New Testament) Alone, out on an island he found the Truth. John saw vividly into the spirit realm.

-Revelations 1:10
"I was in the Spirit on the Lord's Day, and I heard behind me a loud voice like the sound of a trumpet,"

For me, the best description that I can give is seeing under water. The more light shining in on that area gives more detail to the images being seen. That and I see writing, as if it were on a chalkboard or written in a cloud or fog maybe. I saw some man's name written like this once in the fog, it was just the first initial and then as I prayed, the rest of the name came to me. The Lord had a word of encouragement for a total stranger and He wanted me to go and speak with this man's wife! I prayed for 3 days before I called. She was a nurse, and I set up an appointment to speak with her. I told her it was personal and that I would not take much time at all, but I felt that I really needed to speak with her and pray with her. Now, I was unaware what things were taking place on her end of this connection but the Lord knew.

My part in the whole scheme of things was to be obedient and to "go" as I was instructed. I wish I could say that I was brave and fearless and that I stormed right in there with the Word of God, like Samuel would have, without wavering. Instead, I moved in fear and trembling. I wasn't even very confident that I had the name correct. I was going with what I thought I could decipher from the foggy image.

See, I could have let doubts and fear put a halt to my mission, but I pressed on because I went through enough of these instances to recognize my opportunity to step out and exercise my faith. It always feels great after wards when the Lord comes in and sets it all right, even the mishaps of the near miss on the name.

I should tell you that I met this nurse because I was super sick and facing surgery. I was in such bad condition that I was unable to speak, I was barely able to mumble and everyone was doing their best to get through the preliminary to surgery and to get me out of the office. I did not see her again until this meeting that I arranged weeks after the surgery which was almost canceled due to my illness. After the surgery, which was really to determine "if" I had this illness or what was my trouble. That's when the strangest instructions came to me from the Lord, He told me to go in there and get my medical file. He wanted it in hard copy, photos and everything. I called the office to make arrangements. Then after it was set to get my records, I got the foggy image of an "R" and the rest of the name, along with the Rhema Word and instructions to talk to that nurse about her husband. I was also informed that the Lord would heal this ailment in three to five years (sounds a bit like a jail sentence, huh?)

He wanted me to tell 5 people. I guess to make a statement of my belief that He would do this thing and heal my ailment which troubled me for all my life. Wow, so much was riding on this piece of time to step out in faith. You see there was a certain amount of time to carry things out on my end. I can't say what would have happened if I responded differently, or if I would have gotten another chance even. All I knew was that this opportunity was placed before me, right then.

So, when I went to get the records I specifically asked for the one nurse who did my admittance. As I fervently prayed for everything I could think of, little bits of information filtered in. Take this book and that and get a bag... So I put it all together, I kept asking if I had the name correct, which became my fleece. I always was like a Gideon needing my small snippet of proof that God was actually orchestrating the goings on and it wasn't something from my carnal flesh area. I guess if I stopped to think about it, my flesh would have said no way! I am not going on this expedition!

Instead, I went and boy did the Lord show up. HUGE! This sweet woman, I could tell she was just humoring me. Maybe I was humoring the Lord. All I know is that once I came into the office, the whole atmosphere changed.

I purchased my records and was asked to wait in the waiting room for the nurse. She finally brought me into the doctor's office, then she left to take a phone call. I knew she was busy and that I didn't have much time. The familiar weight of an assignment came over me. I shifted into prayer warrior mode. I realized that I was in a place I normally would never have any reason to be. I declared that the land beneath my feet was now taken for the Lord and I looked around the room and began to bless each part of the doctor's office, his chair where he both rested and worked, and his book shelves where he both searched and found answers. For him to be imparted with the Lord's knowledge and for the work of his hands to bring forth the miracles that God wanted in those lives which were placed before this man. All around I prayed, and I asked for victory for the next critical moments that were before me. I could have left at any time, just walked out. Yet, I fought that fear of failure and I stayed.

The nurse returned, and she sat down in front of me. She glanced at my bag. I began with my fleece. "Is your husband's name Robert?" I figured this was as good a place to start as any other.

"No." She told me, but then she said "His name is Rodney, how did you know that?"

I decided Rodney was close enough, and her skepticism seemed to be fading. I could feel the pull of her wanting the rest of the "word" that I told her I had with me. I let it flow out "I have been in prayer for many days now, and I feel that the Lord wants me to share this word with you about your husband, he has been sick and I see his back." Immediately her eyes began to tear up. She was very alert to my words.
"Your husband has a pain in his back, he thinks it will never heal but the Lord is ready to take that from him." With that, she broke into tears and it seemed like she might almost fall off her chair.

There it was, no taking it back now. What was said, could not return void, I had done what the Lord asked of me.

"I want to inform you that the Lord has told me to let 5 people know that He will complete what He has begun and that He will heal your husband and my situation as well (a stomach issue)." I told her all of it, she wept. Then she got up and said she would be right back.

I took my alone time to thank the Lord and to Praise Him for this time and for His healing love. Not too much time passed and the nurse returned, she sat back down and told me that she cleared her schedule. The doctor would not be back for 2 hours and she wanted me to begin again with my word from the Lord, which I gladly shared a second time.

After I did that, she told me that "Rodney" had indeed been in an accident 20 years ago while working on a train track. His back was severely injured and he lived with chronic pain. She, herself was growing very concerned for his health and it was evident that he was giving up on his faith. Even more shocking, he no longer even wanted to live. More and more poured out.

Finally, the bag which I brought came into play. As I shared about the Lord and His healing ways that I had been witness to and the many wonderful things I saw take place, I gave her the materials and explained how to use them. She again cried, because she had gone to 3 churches each a different denomination and sought this kind of help. She wanted to Biblically attack the problems but did not know how. In every instance she was overwhelmingly grateful to what God was doing in all of this.

When I had given her all I carried, and she exhausted her questions, we prayed and I left. I never saw her again and I can only believe that the Lord healed her husband because He healed my ailment in the 3 years of the 3 to 5 that He told me of.

I moved to a whole new state, we were on another journey of Faith to get out of debt. There I was in an entirely new place and needing medical attention again. I brought the records and sure enough, the evidence was absolutely there, the new doctors saw it, confirmed it. The testing began, only something different happened and every time I went in, there was less proof of the problem and more evidence that it was gone! Until the records I now have, clearly show brand new tissue and NO ailment! I have two sets of records, one says illness and the other shows Healed! Amazing! Brand new tissue! This was the only healing that I received which was directly connected to another person. But I have received innumerable healing miracles over the years, and been witness to dozens more in other people.

What I want you to understand is that, even as the events unfold in front of us, it is as if God is behind the scenes working things to our good. We may not see it happening but it is transpiring, almost overlapping what is taking place in the natural. Two things are happening at the same moment in time. This is a Spiritual Realm that runs parallel to our physical realm. It is important to recognize that time doesn't seem to matter in these places. I have seen the Lord move in this space, it is true that God is not bound by the same restrictions to time, that we are bound to. This is because He moves in the Spirit and we have the ability to connect with Him there in that Realm when we ourselves move in Spirit and in Truth.

"But an hour is coming, and now is, when the true worshipers will worship the Father in spirit and truth; for such people the Father seeks to be His worshipers. v.24"God is spirit, and those who worship Him must worship in spirit and truth." ~ John 4:23-24

Push & Pull of the Soul

Now that I have shared what it looks like to see into the Spirit realm (briefly) I want to talk about the natural realm, the one everybody sees and the one we live in each day. Then I can go a little deeper into what I first began sharing, the WAR that we are in. Let me ask you this, did you know that we have 5 senses, we touch, taste, smell, see and hear, right? That is in the natural, but did you know that we have those same 5 senses in this Spiritual Realm? Want to know something else? We have 5 more senses by which to discern our surroundings, and that is in the Soul. I will explain this because most people live their whole lives out and never know they have 15 (fifteen) senses!! Amazing, isn't it? You might be surprised to know that this is just the tip of the iceberg.

As with most of my enlightenment, it comes through the experiences of walking with the Lord each day. I spend time and I 'connect' by reading or listening to the Word and me, I always, always, *always* have worship music going. Even in the children's room, they don't even know that there is another station on the radio! At any moment of the day, I have an unhindered route for the Lord to speak to me. There are many occasions that He has used a story from another believer to stir my heart and quicken my spirit.

If you have never tried this method of complete saturation in the Word, I highly recommend you take up this challenge to only listen to worship music for a month or even two. It is especially critical if you are embarking on the trail of inner healing.

Simply put, garbage in = garbage out. So be cautious of what you put in.

Our soul, is comprised of three compartments. The mind, the will and the emotions. The mind (noe'ma) is where we think up all the false truths that we never take the time to check with the Word of God and make certain that we are on the narrow path. Resulting in being tossed about like one upon the waves. We were given a sound mind, so we need to exercise this and realize our incorrect, learned behaviors can be unlearned.

Our will, is the very same free will that is so critical to our relationship with our Creator. He wants us to desire a fellowship with Him, and would never force this upon us. To love the Lord and want to walk in fellowship with Him is to give over our will and accept the perfect will of God in exchange. In all things saying "Not my will, Lord but yours be done."

Those emotions. They are the wild card in it all. Who can control these? And depending on what is flowing outward, you may not want to hinder the process. Unconditional love from parent to child is an example of emotion that does not need to be bridled. Anger on the other hand can turn deadly. Three areas of vastness to traverse as we go through our lives. Add in other people to the mix and you have countless possibilities for greatness or disaster.

In the book of Ephesians we find an area that gives us a glimpse of a human problem and also offers a solution (which is the way of the Lord). Take note that I say a human problem because it does not matter if you are male or female, old or young. When the devil goes out trapping, he isn't picky. Scripture gives an illustration here.

v.17 This I say therefore, and testify in the Lord, that ye henceforth walk not as other Gentiles walk, in the vanity of their mind, v.18 Having the understanding darkened, being alienated from the life of God through the ignorance that is in them, because of the blindness of their heart: v.19 Who being past feeling have given themselves over unto lasciviousness, to work all uncleanness with greediness. V.20 But ye have not so learned Christ; v.21 If so be that ye have heard him, and have been taught by him, as the truth is in Jesus: v.22 That ye put off concerning the former conversation the old man, which is corrupt according to the deceitful lusts; v.23 And be renewed in the spirit of your mind; ~Ephesians 4:17-23

When Paul talks about the vanity of their minds, he is showing that they are prideful and that they think their thoughts are above that of God's. He says they are ignorant, and further says that they are ignorant because they have deliberately decided not to listen to God (hardened hearts). This attitude alienates us from our Creator. He goes on to say that they have not "learned" Christ, and that explains the ignorance, they just do not know Jesus. V.22 he tells to put off the old man that is the area of the flesh which battles with the soul. V.23 renewing of our minds, this is also addressed in Romans 12:2 and a few more places. It is so important to allow the renewing (washing and restructuring) of our minds. Not in a way contrary to the bible, like hypnosis or tarot cards. I mean allowing your heart and mind to come into obedience of Christ. Surrendering your will for the Perfect Will of God.

Now look at this, verse 24 the second part gives us hope in the solution;

"And that ye put on the new man, which after God is created in righteousness and true holiness."

Just like that! Righteousness and true holiness can be yours! The new man you put on is Christ. It's a choice, to submit to Jesus and follow after Him. Being a Christian isn't for the faint of heart. Believing is faith, and faith is believing. Some things are that simple. Why then, does such a struggle ensue?

Let's look at the scripture in 2Corinthians again, only this time we will add another verse to each end of it. I will separate the verses to further highlight the point that is being made. Watch the wording and follow the way the scripture untwists our natural from the spiritual.

2Corinthians 10:3-6
"For though walking about in the flesh,
we do not war according to the flesh.
For the weapons of our warfare are not carnal,
but mighty through God
to the pulling down of strongholds,
pulling down imaginations
and every high thing that exalts itself against the knowledge of God,
and bringing into captivity every thought into the obedience of
Christ;
And having readiness to avenge all disobedience,
when your obedience is fulfilled."

There is so much information in here!

Walking in the flesh. If you are new to 'church speak' this might seem a bit weird. I will try to explain the meaning. Flesh is a term that we use to describe our "old man" the part of us that died and was buried when we came to Christ.

Daily we fight this flesh, this old man, the old sin nature that we crucified when we made the choice to die to self and live for Christ.

Scripture says this is to "gain" and it is clearly the "better-thing" to choose.

"For to me, to live is Christ and to die is gain."
~Philippians 1:21

A stronghold is any place in your life that the enemy has a foothold and you do not want him there, but he actually has been given a place there, by you. Even if you didn't know it or do it intentionally. This is not the same as "being possessed" A Christian cannot be possessed by a demon. So, don't waste any time being fearful over that. I am talking about things we allow, but these things are not good for us- in physical form (bad eating habits) or in spiritual form (example; pornography) both will in turn affect our soul man (sickness will become evident) The soul is often upset or disturbed by revisiting past hurts. That is why it is critical to healing that we remove (tear down) these disruptions to our inner man.

Remember that our soul has 5 senses too. So if you "hear" an old song, what happens? The memory of that time period when you listened to the song will trigger the emotions associated to that time period. Just as "smells" of a fresh baked pie can trigger memories of say...grandma's house at the holidays. The triggers can be positive or negative. When they are negative and hurtful, it is necessary to up root them. Inner Healing is exactly geared to disarm the power that the enemy has over you through these negative memories. Isn't that a comfort to know, you don't have to stay "stuck" in the muck of your past??

Imaginations. First off, in order to know when something is broken you must first recognize what it should look like while running correctly. Our imaginations are from God, He created us in His image and to His likeness. Jesus is the exact and perfect example that God gave us to follow. He also allows for some pretty amazing stories in the Bible to show examples of others that dealt with similar life situations as we encounter, even now thousands of years later. People are people wherever you go, you're going to hear me say that a lot because it never stops being true.

A few years back, I made up a bedtime prayer for my boys. They always were asking for me to pray for them to have "good dreams" and seemed to fret much less if I covered this in the prayer. They would ask to have anointing oil on their little noggins before they could sleep. We prayed this way for about ten years. The prayer goes like this: "Bad dreams go, and good dreams come, In the Name of Jesus. My thoughts are good and my heart is good, and my imagination is pure and holy. I belong to Jesus and He belongs to me. Bad dreams go and good dreams come, In the Name of Jesus." That's it! They needed to know that they had the power to disarm the enemy and have a good night's rest. The Bible tells us that "You will lie down in peace and your sleep will be sweet." This prayer and the oil gave them peace, and they slept.

Our imagination is a beautiful gift from God, I think we should use it more and not try to stifle it and suppress it, to conform to others guidelines. Kids should day dream and even adults too!! However, when the imagination, the "sanctified" imagination is not given over to the Blood of Jesus, that is when the enemy can gain access and give those bad thoughts a playground. Have you ever wondered why bad things happen to good people? This is an area where bad thoughts were allowed to flourish in an un-checked, un-sanctified imagination. The result is sin and usually some kind of outward act against the natural ways of righteousness. In other words, we have the choice to make of what we will allow our thoughts to think on. If you have imaginations that are against being good & holy, those would need to be washed in the Blood of Jesus and "pulled down". Not difficult at all, once you recognize what thoughts do not belong and you decide to "resist the devil".

> *"Submit yourself therefore to God,*
> *resist the devil and he will flee."*

To bring something into captivity is a lot like this "pulling down" which I just addressed. You must identify the thought (many times over in a day if need be) and you grab it and say, "No!" you are not good and I will not think on you. Then you take a scripture that you know is good and you switch this out with your bad thought.

Here is an example; you are at the grocery store and you have a confrontation with someone who has 65 items and is clearly not sup-posed to be in the 10 item lane. You look at the cart. They start swearing at you, and give lots of attitude. Do you cuss them out? How do you handle that? Personally, I try to be patient, I figure they know how to count, so they must have chosen to get in this lane to further speed up their departure, so I wouldn't engage. I wouldn't let them pull me into their frenzied state of mind. Not because I can't think up a string of rude comments, but rather because I feel like they might just need a break. Maybe a smile and hey, if I have a coupon I'd probably give that to them as well. It's true, my kids have seen this play out. In this whole situation, both sides have choices to make.

Mercy and grace are given freely and in heaping doses from God to us all day long, maybe He wants some of it to flow through you and out into the world that is right before you.

Now, let's take all the things that were addressed here and realize that each day, each moment affects our soul. Our inner man. We feel and we respond to feelings, we allow them to lead us. Sometimes on to paths that are not good to be on. Paths of anger and revenge to name a couple. This is the push and the pull of our soul. No matter what life situation you are in, you always have a choice. Even if the choice is only in HOW you will respond. How you will react to what has hap-pened or is happening.

One day we will all stand before the Lord and give an account of our lives. He will not ask what has been done to you, and how would you like me to avenge it for you. He will ask, did you love the unlova-ble? Did you clothe the poor and give food to the hungry? Did you forgive the unforgivable? Did you follow the example I gave you in Je-sus? Because Jesus loved and forgave, which means we have it in us to do the same. You will never be asked to give an account for what hap-pened to you, but only for what you chose to do with what happened to you. I find rest in knowing that God does see it all and that He knows how to work it all too good.

Quickly, we must realize that the enemy sees it too, because he rec-ognizes Christ, the anointed One. Therein lies the WAR. It's the age old battle for our soul. Each time you shine like Jesus, you shine a bright light into darkness, and darkness will look and search for ways that it can "buddy up" with you, which in turn leads to him trying to turn that shining beacon off. "The thief comes to steal, kill and destroy."

You are his mission and your destruction is his only aim. Does that make you mad? I hope so, because that is a holy anger to want to stand against the whiles of the devil. We are to hate what God hates but love what God loves. God loves people, His children, but He hates the sin nature. He knows what evil does, that is why He cast it out of Heaven. There could be no evil in Heaven and pride was the number 1 culprit, so long ago. Do you think that "pride" isn't one of satan's best tools to use against us? What about music? You know he was in charge of worship, the most holy worship in Heaven. How beautiful it would be to hear those sounds, and yet he turned against God and thought he knew better than his Creator. It is dangerous territory to tread.

Here is the thing, when we act in ways that are contrary to God, we are acting out of the sin nature and that nature is easily recognized by the enemy. This is because those are his characteristics. So if you act, say resentful, then who would you think you are drawing towards you? A Holy God that forgives or a spiteful snake that is bent on revenge? See, that is the game that the devil plays. Can I get the believer to stumble? Can I get him/her to gossip about another? Could I stir strife and bring offense? Those are the thoughts of the enemy towards us. Why do we give him a place? I know it can be easier sometimes to just go with your feelings, but I tell you the truth those feelings can be rooted in old negative mindsets and not good for your future.

I have been talking about this **flesh**, this thing we fight and must learn that it is part of us, yet we are the master and it is the servant. The flesh, is the first line of defense and the first to be attacked by our enemy. Once the enemy can break past your flesh, he can then seep into those thoughts and gain access into the soul realm, which can then lead to affecting your spirit. It is like a bad fungus that you just can't kill. How does it happen? How does a Holy temple (the body) have sin and corruption?

I'm glad you asked.

Real Life Situations

It always helps me a great deal to have some guidelines. Maybe I learn by example just as much as I learn by doing. Experience being the best teacher and all. You may never have even heard of soul wounds, but that doesn't mean they aren't taking place. I'll bet you recognize them as you read on.

"Above all else, guard your heart, for it is the wellspring of life."
Proverbs 4:23

Remember that patterns of thought tend to lead to patterns of speech - issues of the heart, flow from the mouth. It is safe to say that if it's inside you, then it will flow out of you. Through your speech or an attitude or through withholding your affections towards others. When your heart is hurting, you don't want to be nice, and God knows this. He understands that the heart and the mind are potentially a breeding ground for the darkness. We think on a thing (ruminating as Peter calls it) then we cultivate it in our heart, next thing you know, we are talking and acting out this new frustration that should have been "taken captive" much sooner than it was.

This is also parallel to prayer. A healthy prayer life, is time spent with Father God, every day. Why? Because every day we are bombarded with issues, offenses or hurts that affect our heart and mind. When you go straight to prayer as the first reaction, then you get God's perspective on the incident and He can keep you on that narrow path. By coming to Jesus first thing in prayer, you foil the enemy's plans! You immediately come under the protection of the Lord and a hedge is placed around about you.

What does the other side of it look like? You spout off and send forth negative words, hacking and slashing at another brother or sister in the Lord. Now you can't take it back and the destruction can be devastating for years to come. But you wouldn't really care about that would you, because you "got even". You got them good. And I'll have you know, that revenge was your only reward for what you did. That satisfaction of getting even. However the Lord would have rather you walked the road of forgiveness and love. Applying mercy & grace just as you want for yourself. Now your situation is much worse and to set it right, you have to go and deliver yourself to the judge.

You'll not only have to apologize to God but you will have to apologize to that person(s) whom you so eloquently told off. Hmmm, how it would have been easier to just clamp it down and take it into prayer. See?

Even now, right now as you read this, if something is coming to your mind that should be taken into prayer and covered with the BLOOD of Jesus, then I implore you to set aside the time and make the necessary amends. You will be glad that you did, and you'll be a better person for it.

The Deepest Wounds

Have you ever read the biblical account of Tamar? I'm referring to the story in 2 Samuel 13. This is not the same account of Tamar from the book of Genesis chapter 38. There were two women and each has quite a story to tell. I cover Tamar's story from Genesis in the 3rd book of this series. Today I would like to address the tragic and heart breaking account of the rape which took place in King David's household. The incident involved his children and the damage of such an act left wide spread effects, carrying on for years.

Let's bring this a little closer to home. I want to present a hypothetical situation, this is completely made up and in no way represents anyone that I have been in prayer ministry with.

Let's say that there is a
Woman...
Loves the Lord
Working in the Kingdom
Raised by Godly parents
(Appearance is unassuming)
She accompanies her husband on Missionary Trips

One evening this Hypothetical woman goes out to the market, to get some ice-cream.

She and her husband just returned from an extended trip to a 3rd world country—that does not have ice-cream. She goes out alone to

buy some. All of a sudden, she is attacked, knocked- out, and raped.
Q. Now I ask you what part of her was attacked (?)
-Her temple (body)
Q. What was it that violated this woman? Good or Evil?

When she comes to, no one is around, no one at all.
Pulling herself together she seeks treatment and files a police report.

Because she did not see who her attacker was, there is no way for the authorities to find this man. They would like to help, but they just can't.

So she goes home and gets on with her life....
But she can't sleep at night. The instance haunts her. Every time she closes her eyes she is tormented by the memories. It is as if she is right back in the moment.

Terrified to sleep she begins to take pills to stay awake.
The Strongman comes, and he begins to build his house.

Scriptural Reference: Tamar and her brother Amnon. Long story short Amnon forces Tamar to lay with him, then he kicks her out adding insult to injury and she tears her robe and puts ashes on her head. She does try to stop him and reason with him.

> *(2Sa 13:13) And I, where shall I cause my shame to go?*

> *(2Sa 13:14) But he would not listen to her voice; but being stronger than she, he forced her and lay with her.*

The thief will (violate) anyway he can
Comes but to steal, kill and destroy.
Violate your temple with cigarettes
Drugs
Alcohol
He too is no respecter of persons.

What these two women have in common is that they were not looking for this to happen, they did not go out in search of it... it was DONE to them.

Strongman (is the thief)
Violated her temple (body)
Shame and guilt enter
> [Deeper into the temple...]
> [Into the soul realm]

She is afraid to leave her house
> [The root of Bitterness has sprung up]

She is probably angry
Angry at the one who attacked her, sure.
But maybe even angry at herself, for allowing it to happen. (Lie of the emery)

Maybe she is even mad at the God she loves and trusted...
The if- only's now enter into her mind.
The 'WHY ME???' (Pride accompanied by shame)
It builds....

Time passes, one year, two years
She no longer goes on the missionary trips because fear grips her heart every time she tries to leave her house.

[Hate enters]
She hates the man that hurt her, who stole her freedom and so much more.
[Deeper into the soul]
> [Depression sets in]

The Strongman builds
She knows if she ever saw that man again she would kill him for what he did, maybe she even prays for him to die
[Deeper still into her soul
She makes a vow for revenge
  Spirit is affected]

Vows stop the flow of God in our lives.

She is "Bound"

In every way this woman is "Bound."
Body/ Soul/ Spirit

What can free her???

Of course the only answer is Jesus!
But even before He comes in and cleans up the mess, the wake of destruction from the enemy. A choice needs to be made by the individual that has been wronged. (Free will)

The decision to forgive.

The most powerful assault against our enemy is forgiveness.
Freedom comes through this choice. Forgiving the attacker, and also forgiving herself.

Confessing her feelings, (emotions). Repenting for taking on the false identity and releasing the whole thing to God.

As a side note, I know that it might seem un-fair that she would have to repent, since she was the victim. However, in several instances this woman took on the characteristics of the enemy. Hate, anger, bitterness etc. Can you go through and identify those areas?

Let's keep going, and I hope that you see there is no room for the devil in our lives.

We have to say "The gates of hell shall not prevail."

How the Enemy Enters

By now it should be getting clearer that you are being watched and targeted. The arrow that flies by night and the wolf in sheep's clothing, or the lion that is roaming about, but is not exactly a lion, yet he circles and watches, looking for an opportunity to pounce. 1Peter states that he looks to devour.

Look at this scripture in Genesis 4:7 states this...

"If you do what is right, won't you be accepted? But if you do not do what is right, sin is crouching at the door. Its desire is for you, but you must rule over it."

Crouching at your door, slunk down and foaming at the mouth. Hungrily desiring your slip up. Sin, watches and waits. For what? It is waiting for you to make a move, any move that it can identify with. When you act in a manner that is contrary to God's character, then the sin finds a way to "partner" with you and comes near in the situation; as much as you allow. Let's use worry for an example, worrying can turn into full blown fear. The enemy loves fear and will recognize it and begin to whisper more words of worry/fear towards you. More thoughts of impending doom, and you can quickly let the dread of it all carry you right off.

The scripture says you must rule over it. Not that you should try or you might succeed, it states that you must rule over it. That you can and you should be the master of it. If God tells you that you must do something, then that is the very thing He will empower you to do. Yet, it can be difficult to stand up and fight if you are cowering in fear and confusion. This is where scripture memorization can really come in handy. You need to own the Words of God that comfort and empower your spirit man. These will become the sword that cuts out what does not belong.

Wounded Soldiers

I can't help it, sometimes I think of God's children like little soldiers, wounded from battle and unaware of how to get to the hospital. Their training long since forgotten. If only they knew...

Life can be harsh and navigation can seem treacherous at times. There certainly are storms and there's a whole lot of ups and downs. But when were we ever promised to skate on through without so much as a scuff mark? What would be the purpose of the Full Armor of God if we weren't engaging in a battle? The whole point of the fight is to allow us a choice. The choice to pick which side we want to be on. Of course Jesus is on the winning team, but getting ourselves fully wrapped up in that concept can be difficult.

Once the soul has taken damage, it can be years before anything is even done about it. You limp along and nurse your wounds and hope that you can get over it, eventually. Likelihood of it disappearing overnight is pretty small. You need to face it, own it and then take care of it. That is when your soul will find the soothing Balm of Gilead.

Downward Spiral of Rejection

This has been a weighty block of text already and consumption can be difficult, I understand that there have been many areas covered. You may even feel a bit like you have been poked and prodded, that is the Holy Spirit testing and checking. It's a good thing. Taking all of that into consideration, I still feel that I would be remiss if I did not address one of the ugliest and most destructive emotions. Rejection.

We reject others, we reject ourselves and we reject God's salvation.

I stood in the place of a prodigal for far too long. Can you imagine, I had the audacity to speak directly to God and engage in conversations with Him almost daily, yet I would not bend my knee because I believed that He had wronged me? I didn't trust Him either, being the "authority figure" and for a whole bunch of years I felt like I was on the outside, peeking in the windows at all the other Christians, but I never felt like I could come into the fellowship. I was an outsider. That made me angry. I felt like I had a stamp of rejection on my forehead. I couldn't figure out why Jesus kept pursuing me if He had already rejected me. I can laugh now at how far off I was in my assumptions. Every time people failed me, I blamed God. He never planned for me to go into foster care or for my husband to die and leave me a widow with two children. He never planned on any of the hurtful and traumatic incidents that I lived through. He did plan to love me and be patient with me while I figured out that He was the only one who could repair my broken heart and that He was the only one that actually wanted to! Even in my wandering, He extended mercy and grace to me.

Rejection is seemingly an external attack. In actuality, it is really most detrimental because it turns internally. At some point if you wallow in the emotion of allowing others to reject you and you take that on, it changes from being their voices you hear and one day you realize that the only voice spraying poison at you, is you. Your own rejection turns to self-hatred. You become your own accuser, bringing down the sentence and punishment upon yourself. Where can you turn when this happens? What escape is there from your own self?

For me, it wasn't until I was about 33 that anyone actually told me that I could attend a different church besides the Catholic Church that I had been part of most of my life. As an adult for 12 years I attended and took my children. I have many memories of my grandma Jeannette taking me to church when I was a young girl. She and I spent time together walking across the town and over through some apple trees by way of a small dusty footpath. Grandma loved Jesus, but she was bound by the rules of our household and she had to take us to a Catholic church. I know now that she figured out, any church is better than No church at all.

When I did gain an understanding that it was okay to attend a Pentecostal, Spirit Filled church I was forever changed. Those feelings of being on the outside began to diminish. I was Free to Know Jesus, and this gave me the greatest joy!! It took some time before the hollow religious spirit was broken off. I took everything that the Lord offered to me, and most of it came through other obedient servants to Christ. I began to love and receive love. Step by step I began to walk in the Lord, until I could start my steady jogging, as I began to run the race of faith. Strength coming to me in the trials and opportunity after opportunity to exercise my faith. I won't even entertain the thoughts of where I would be or what would have become of me, if I had not gone through that growing season.

When the news came to me that my beautiful son Justin had followed in his father's footsteps and had taken his own life, I was once again that small and helpless girl, feeling alone and abandoned. Fortunately, it didn't last long and I found a new way to hide in the Lord, I began another season of growth. This time I was equipped with all that Jesus had been pouring into me. All the sharpening and the hours of studying which I thought was for the classes I taught, but it was for fortifying my position and preparing me for the biggest battle of my life.

Once again the devil circled around me and tried his tricks, he played the same cards that were dealt out before. He tried the guilt and the self-blame, he offered up death as an option and of course rejection was on the docket too. It was as if an invisible hole in the earth had opened up and I was standing at the threshold. I could feel the heat and I knew from experience that the furnace can go 7 times hotter. I wanted no part of it.

The irony and the solution of all the death and pain; love. The way to fight this invisible enemy was with the most powerful tool that I possess and that is love. To stay in the position that I fought so hard to be in. Washed and sanctified in the Blood of the Most Holy One. Jesus never left my side. He has been steadfast and oh so trustworthy through it all.

It hurts me inside to think on the way I used to be. So afraid and completely immobilized by all my fears and misguided thoughts. Raised in an ungodly home and fighting the memories. I hope that sharing a little of my story can give you a portion of strength it will now take to make your stand. I will show you now, how to recognize rejection and what to do when you see it. Let me encourage you in this, once you call upon the Name of Jesus to help you in this battle, you should never quit. You should purpose in your heart to never go backwards, as the Lord only moves in a forward direction as we are walking out our salvation.

There is a truth here that you must own and be diligent to hold on to. Everything that the Lord does is good. He fights for us, and no matter the situation He is on our side 110%. He is all in. This piece of understanding took me through many trials, it was like a life raft in the storms. No matter what was thrown at me, I knew He was good and that He would work things to (towards) good. I bring this up because not everything that you are asked to do will be easy.

"These are the words of him who is holy and true, who holds the key of David. What he opens no one can shut, and what he shuts no one can open." [~Jesus] book of Revelations 3:7

This scripture is designed to give you fortitude. An assurance that the one who is holy and true (Jesus) holds the key. The keys to hell and death are His as well, but I always felt this scripture to have personal ring to it. I won't get into it much now but if you back up a few verses to 2:10 it is very personal and I feel like this verse here just continues on as he speaks to me. That being said, I feel what John wants us to know is that if Jesus closes a door per say or an avenue or cuts something off, He is doing it for good. He is doing it intentionally and He is making sure it will not come around again! I can follow along and see that the same holds true if he opens up something towards us, or for us or in spite of us.

Meditate on this scripture. Say it, and as you do, begin to ask the Lord what He wants you to shut the door on? And what does He want you to cut off? A job, a relationship, perhaps a friendship that is unhealthy? Is there an area in your life that you feel like you are in a tug-of-war with God? If you say yes to that, then I encourage you to start with this point. Prayer and even fasting can remove any obstacles and bring you Freedom.

Here is a small checklist of questions that I sense could bring you to a new understanding of what is happening inside of you. Remember that Jesus says this:

"I have come that they may have life, and have it to the full."
—John 10:10

- Life is too hard and painful
- There's no point in trying
- God won't hear my prayer if there is sin in my heart, so why bother to pray?
- Nobody understands me
- I can't do anything right
- Everybody is smarter than I am
- Nobody believes me
- I am just dirt under their feet
- I can never trust Jesus
- He will send me to hell.
- I have nothing to offer
- I'm hopeless
- I'm ugly

- I'm not worth anything
- I don't deserve anything anyway

Okay, that was 15 items. How many did you circle?? There is not a right and wrong situation here. This little piece of homework was for you to check your own soul and see if wounds are present. The full checklist is at my website: www.scarsofsuicide.com

There are no issues which are isolated. All of this is common to man, and all of it can be put under your feet, so don't lose heart. We all have to begin some place. Just begin.

As a last note, I'd like to leave you with these memorization scriptures: As you discover a rejection issue, apply one of these scriptures to it. Cast down the negative thought, and tell it to go and do not return. Do all these things **IN the NAME of JESUS!**

I_____ have value.
    "Look at the birds of the air: they neither sow nor reap nor gather into barns, and yet your heavenly Father feeds them. Are you not of more value than they?" -Mathew 6:26

I_____ walk in new life. "Therefore we were buried with Him by baptism into death, in order that, just as Christ was raised from the dead by the glory of the Father, so we too may walk in a new way of life." –Romans 6:4

I _____ am presented to God, holy and Blameless.
                    –Colossians 1:22

I_____ am loved, and wanted.
    For He shall give His angels charge over thee, to keep thee in all thy ways. –Psalm 91:11

Pray all things believing in God's Righteous Right Hand.
The Name of JESUS never fails <3

Reach Higher-Dig Deeper

Reach Higher- Dig Deeper

This should be our pursuit of the Lord.

Temporary Comforts (the nice houses etc. later on are seen as the Tree which grew to shade Jonah)

Given by God's Mercy to get us through, even if it has no eternal value in the big picture.

What matters?

What Doesn't?

Let's take a minute to talk about word curses and what that means in the "Big Picture" of life.

Pertaining to the things of God, I was so clueless. I am serious, if ever there were a time of complete confusion; it was during this stretch of highway; my teenage years. Some of you know what I mean and I am sure there are readers who did have life figured out. I am talking to the former, not the latter.

I was clueless. In so many ways, and my focus was very askew.

If only someone would have told me things that could have changed my life, I was searching but the Lord remained a mystery.

The *Victim*- I never wanted to be her. The one that always stayed, no matter what.

The saying "What you don't know, won't hurt you." That is so untrue. In my life I have found that knowledge is power. It is beneficial to making educated decisions and leading a Spirit Filled life. To not know can be detrimental to a person that is lost. This is why it is so critical for those that Do Know Jesus Christ to share this information with those that have not yet met Him. It is also very important for those that are older and wiser to train the younger generation. Passing on wisdom is a gift that is too often mistaken for pride or judgment. Search as I might, my memory comes up short on women who guided me or cared enough to take even a moment to give wisdom.

I never heard the term "Word Curses" before I was an adult and regularly attending church. Immediately I understood the concept and I fully embraced the route to healing from the destruction which follows being called names and being made to feel worthless.

I began to realize that when my parents yelled their curses at me, it was not really the voice of my father or mother but the voice I was hearing was their own fear speaking and their own self-hatred.

The Lord began to show me that my parent's insecurities and their own low self- image were the real words I was hearing while they tore me down.

You can't give away what you do not possess. They did not have an infilling of love, which is a result of knowing Jesus.

If you have suffered from the negative effects of ill-willed people speaking foul things at you, remember Jesus died to take those from you too.

-In prayer, speak them out, and release them to Him.

-Forgive the offending party and hold them accountable no longer.

Freedom comes on the wings of forgiving...

Forgiving is so important that Jesus died on a cross to make a way for you to return to God when you die. That is what forgiveness looks like from a loving Father, He will do everything to ensure your rightful place with Him.

The Onion Effect

I have heard it explained to me in a similar way in the church I attended when I lived in Alaska. The onion effect I have named it. Things around this church were deeply geared towards climbing to the Mountain of God and finding Freedom in Christ. My husband and I joined a small group, it didn't stay small for long, before we knew it nearly all the church was attending the Monday night (free of charge) meetings. We would hear an hour or so of testimony and then another hour of teaching, or instead of teaching you could join a smaller group that met in another room. The turnout was incredible, and there eventually had to be folks in the parking lot directing traffic which filled up the two tier parking. It was a packed house.

I went through the prayer counseling that was offered by scheduled groups for 10-12 weeks at a time. My prayer leader put me in two groups back to back. I was gaining ground like nobody's business. When I grasped what was going on in the healing realms, I was like a junkie for the Holy Spirit. I couldn't get enough.

Well, anyway during this amazing growing season it was explained that the "gunk" (I will call it) comes off in pieces or in LAYERS like an onion has those layers on it. It's a pretty good description too because as you peel away at the onion it can make you cry. For me, I nearly passed out once from the overwhelming presence of the Holy Ghost coming in and pulling at my layers surrounding my 1st husband's death by suicide. I thought I was easing into this group and my plan was to wait it out in the back row (so to speak) and easy-peasy I would just have a look around. HA! The Lord wasn't having any of that. Just think for a moment what was involved and all the moving and job contracts and shuffling it took to place me in Alaska, where this sort of thing was available? The Lord went to great lengths to orchestrate it all.

What I was sitting there guarding and protecting (the pain and shame of it all) the Good Lord was trying to help me get free of it! So, as the prayer counselor began to share how her first husband died and that she was left with a small child and all that, I literally felt like the walls were closing in and the room started to go black. Maybe I was holding my breath or maybe I nearly fainted, I don't really know but it grabbed a hold of me and would take all the faith I had to keep coming back week after week. For two groups and then another 12 or so more weeks to take their prayer counseling from the church.

Once I was in it, I was committed to pushing past the fear of all that I had to deal with. Look at how amazing the Holy Spirit is! Not only did I deal with my own onion layers of stinky gunk, I was privileged to witness dozens of others shake free of their chains as well! What an honor to be part of such a stream of cleansing. I will always be grateful for the work that the Holy Spirit did during those years in Alaska, and grateful to the many seasoned prayer warriors that the Lord surrounded me with. I was protected while I fell apart and loved while I was put back together by the Potter's hands.

As with anything that the Lord does, He can perform miracles and take all your layers in one swoop of His Mighty Hand. You might think that sounds nice, and boom you would be healed of a life's worth of heartache. I actually think that He doesn't do this very often, for a reason. Could we ever really appreciate something if it cost us nothing? If your healing is worth anything, then it would have to bear a value. What about the value of time invested? Could the cost, simply come down to your perseverance and your own commitment to change your lifestyle? That is a cost, in giving up TV viewing for time to soak in the Word or even to listen to music on You-tube. That is a Blessing I have now, but did not have when I went through the first decade of healing with Jesus.

What about the tough one, like giving up friends or family members that laugh at you for wanting to go to church, or accuse you of having a boyfriend and not really going to church for that many hours. If you are in the right kind of church, then you know that the real church goes on after church service is over, or when you've met the Lord at the altar and time loses all significance.

There is a man in the Bible who said:

"I will not give to the Lord, that which cost me nothing."
I want you to consider it an assignment to find out who said this and what was he talking about. What did he give? Once you figure it out, then go the next step and read about this man's life. He was no stranger to the ups and downs of the emotions which flood us today. This man can teach us a whole lot about God's love towards us.

There are exchanges In Christ, which do not even feel like enough of a price was paid (on our end) Think about what was nailed to the cross, does it seem like an even exchange that I give my sorrow for what Jesus gave me? I know God will always out give whatever I bring to the table. As I write these books, I ponder this point. One such instance that I could share here is the request made by the Lord one morning, He simply asked me not to read any other books while I was writing. Just stop, cold turkey and only read from the Bible. I did sneak in a couple magazines on house decorating, but I felt like it was not a deal breaker because that glancing and daydreaming are my fluffy activity, which gives my mind a rest as it wanders and ponders...

I have bookshelves full of materials, I absolutely love to read. I have various magazine subscriptions and friends even send me books that they enjoyed and want to share with me. I could read none of it. About a year after my son died did this request come forth. I thought no big deal. It even seemed strange to ask such a thing.

But as the months wore on, I really began to miss my books. I got to a point where I packed them into bins and pushed them into the closet because they tempted me. Just a quick peek Lord! Can't I flip through the pages of those brand new books I received for Christmas?? I allowed myself the few that were more reference materials, the ole' dictionary and thesaurus. The Nelson's Bible dictionary and the Archaeological Bible (maps and such!) I kept handy the Interlinear Bible that was given as a birthday gift (I actually begged for this one!) things like this I kept out, but the rest I have not touched, although I do move things around a bit and look at the covers... soon I know the time is coming soon.

I am approaching the four year anniversary of my son's death by suicide. My deepest and most peculiar healing season. What I know now, is much different than when I began the journey. At first I was just pouring it all out in my journals. Then after year one the Lord said, now write that book... The "book" became so big that I could not call it a book anymore, it was colossal. Every day, as I walked with the Lord, He shared so much that I could not even write it out fast enough! I started speaking to my phone in the small hours of the morning and sending it to my emails and then over to my scrivener program (a tool I won in a writing contest along the way) I have spent the last year and a half wading and sorting through the sheer volume of what I was shown, and healing along the way, in small steady doses.

He didn't want me reading other people's work because He wanted HIS voice to come through (and I pray that has happened) He wanted me to get out of the way and let Him do the work He began so long ago. I gave up the books, but I got so much more in return! I have to break down the teachings because I do not even have words to place on the Supernatural experiences that transpired. My human limitations will never meet the level that the Lord is at. I am trying though, because I realize that what He shared with me, isn't just for me. Other people will want to know these things too.

The books weren't the only thing I gave up. We lost our church about a year after my son died and then they completely shut the door on us 6 months later. It was a painful time, and I was devastated. As I approached the three year mark of no church, the Lord did open up a place for us to go, where we were not judged by the outward and were much more easily accepted because of our relationship with Christ. I don't want to speak negative about the church, we are all on different levels as we walk with our Jesus; in the end it was better for me to just be "alone" with the Lord as He did His miracles in my heart. He has worked it out to good, just as the scripture promised.

I could not have gone through what I did with any human person as my crutch, I found that I could only lean upon the Lord for He was the only one able to bear the weight of the Suicide that I had to learn to live with as my new reality. Jesus never took anything away that He didn't replace with something far better.

I also lived off the grid during this time, a choice that my husband and I made about a year and 1/2 before we lost our Justin. During an accident with a saw, Michael lost two of his fingers and the building project drastically lost momentum as he was out of work for the injury, but when Justin died *all* the wind went out of our sails. The world stopped moving, until such time that the Lord jump started me again.

I worked by flashlight for about 75% of everything I have written and transferred over to the laptop which my dear husband purchased because it had an extended battery life. For the rest of the power I go off of solar, or my little battery (from a 4-wheeler) that has an inverter humming along as I move through the process of turning my experience into written form. I thought I was just documenting for my children, but the Lord had other plans I guess.

I gave up people too. I love people and interacting with them. For these "writing" years I have been out here on a remote road with not so much as a street sign. Left at the fork, to the dead end. Today I can say, it brings me such joy living in complete reliance on Jesus for all my needs. **I truly live on the road less traveled!**

I say **"I healed among the trees"** that is how I see it. Coming from a gated community 45 minutes from Chicago where I was born, yes, you could say this was a transformation. A time of changes in large and small doses. I like to think of it as the Lord's polishing.

"I healed among the wind" in the trees, there were many days that I heard the voice of the Lord in the rustle of those trees. We heat our house with these same trees. We bathe in rain water that is provided, even in the middle of winter. It is harvested and filtered.

We have not lacked for anything. People's reactions vary to finding out that we live remotely and that I am very active on the Internet.

I pray with others all around the world, but I do it through Skype or Zoom etc. We have 4G wireless service, but when you leave my driveway it is gone. I stay on this narrow path, because the Lord is here and I don't want to walk away from Him.

I am isolated or *insulated* from the world. You could look at it either way. I think of it as a protective cocoon, just surrounded by the things of God as I finish what He called me to do.

At first I felt like I was forgotten out here in the middle of nowhere. He sent us here, there is no doubt about that. I know He always was aware of my whereabouts, I had to get an understanding of His. So He stripped away the distractions and He pulled me into a quiet place, alone with Him so that He could minister to my deepest needs. What love! What amazing Love He has lavished on me!

You can have new life too, and let the struggles with your past fall away like the leaves fall in the autumn as winter approaches. What you fear now, can be turned into your greatest triumph in the Christ.

"I will not give to the Lord, that which cost me nothing...."

Never were these words truer than in the raw emotion of my heartache as I lost my son to suicide.

There is a biblical principle to which the law of reaping and sowing would apply here in my life. As I sowed in my heart's cry for this enormous loss, I could place it nowhere else but into the arms of My Savior. I could not hold what was more than I could bear, and I wasn't being asked too either. In the longing for peace to come once again into my soul and for the love I had towards my son, not desiring that love be turned to bitterness, I surrendered my anguish at the foot of the cross. I sowed in the seed of my son unto the Lord. I gave him over in life and also in his death.

What-so-ever Jesus decides to do with this seed and how He wants to grow this, and to whatever it may turn out to be, I place all of those dreams into His hands as well.

If you are reading this type of book because you too, have lost your family member to the spirit of suicide and find yourself in the tsunami of pain; these bits of guidance are the best that I can offer. I extend them to you and I truly believe that you can be whole again and functioning on the highest levels. Life in the pit of darkness and regret do not have to be your fate.

Prayer Portions

Let your prayers be towards strengthening yourself to withstand the task of the "Onion Effect". To stay the course as you see this through. You will go deeper where the inner parts are softer, fleshly. This is the area that will cause you to reconsider what you have started because it can be uncomfortable to face the things you have stuffed down into your soul's closets. It is time for a deep clean. Think of it as a deliberate taking back of the ground stolen from you. As you clear out the "Spiritual Clutter" you will be making room for the Holy Ghost to come in and be bigger than ever in your life. Every time you pay the cost of bearing your cross, you will find that Jesus has a way of giving back more than what you gave up or gave over to Him.

He will not leave you disappointed!

Crawl up on the lap of Jesus and let Him peel away those layers. Rest in the safety of His arms and begin to enjoy the effect of healing your wounded soul. Trust that He has you where you need to be in order to receive the next piece of what He has for you.

Fear not.

God has said, *"Never will I forsake you." So, we say with confidence, "The Lord is my helper; I will not be afraid. What can man do to me?" ~Hebrews 13:5-6*

Using scripture to change your perspective, allow these words to wash over you and to take hold of your new way to understand and be part of God's good plan for you.

Fear none of those things which thou shalt suffer: behold, the devil shall cast some of you into prison, that ye may be tried; and ye shall have tribulation ten days: be thou faithful unto death, and I will give thee a crown of life. ~Revelation 2:10

Because the foolishness of God is wiser than men; and the weakness of God is stronger than men. ~1Corinthians 1:25

Light is sown for the righteous, and gladness for the upright in heart. ~Psalms 97:11

For I will be merciful to their unrighteousness, and their sins and their iniquities will I remember no more. ~Hebrews 8:12

Father God, help the renewing of my mind and the rebuilding of my broken heart. My trust is in You for I believe that you are well able to restore what has been robbed from me and to place me among the upright. I desire the gladness that only Your love can provide. On my own Lord, I am too weak and I do not have the wisdom to be successful, but with You on my side I can accomplish all that You purpose for me and even more than I could dream or imagine. Help me Jesus to be better tomorrow than I am today. I trust You with my life and I believe You're the answer to all of my troubles. Deliver me now from the evil ways of my enemy. Bless me Lord and I will be blessed. And I pray all of these things in Jesus precious and Holy Name. The Name above all Names. Forever, Amen.

Jesus will prevail and all that He has sent out towards your bright future will shine radiantly through His life within your life.

CHAPTER THREE

BLOODline Plumbline

Quest for Nobility

There is something in us all which desires to be more. One look at our society and it becomes obvious that we are a driven people. It goes all the way back to Adam & Eve. You see the corrupt nature begin to show as the first two inhabitants of God's creation decide in their own hearts that they need more. Sure, we can look back and say that they should have been content with what they had. They did in fact have it all! There was nothing they lacked nor wanted for, as Father God did provide everything in that Garden of Eden. Yet, upon first opportunity, the doubts came in... Maybe something is being withheld from us?

Taking without asking, they acquired what it was they longed for. **More.**

Are we so different now? What if we could be content with what we have? How would life be if we did not covet nearly every day, longing for the bigger, faster, better whatever? If we were honest, we would say that no matter how much we gained, our insatiable appetite for power would not be satisfied still.

Here's the irony, we have what Adam & Eve had. Jesus took back the victory that Adam lost and we, now today live and breathe and walk in the freedom that was lost in the garden God gave to man, so long ago. Life to the fullest, abundant life. Man had it, lost it and now through Christ regains it again. Why is it we still want more?

I believe it comes down to significance. We never quite feel worthy and there seems to always be a nagging suspicion that we can't ever measure up. On some level we do not feel like we have the extravagant significance that we truly do have. Striving to get more and to fill the voids within our hearts. Our thoughts and attitudes are driven by our desires and the decisions we make are directly connected to our issues in life which then shape our beliefs. In other words, one thing affects another and if none of the things are led by the truth in the word of God, we will have a mess to deal with. What is the flip side to that? Our relationship with Jesus has to be positioned correctly (lining up with the WORD) in order for us to fully be fulfilled. Jesus satisfies all of the desires of our hearts.

When you look around at your circumstances you might think, I don't feel fulfilled and I sure don't feel significant. You then might be just the one that this is written for. I can say that because the truth meant for you has been covered by your doubts and perhaps even some skepticism of the Lord to do what He promises. It's in us all to wonder if there is more, that is why God dealt with the issue first thing, right from the get-go. In every instance of the weakness we hold the potential to perform, God brought about a situation that allowed us to deal with that weakness.

In order to reveal it to us and then to remove it from us.

So, what's the catch? We have to want to be purified. We have to desire to be washed in the Blood and cleansed by the rivers of Living Water and even when necessary brought through the fires of purification.

"But He knows the way I take; When He has tried me, I shall come forth as gold." -Job 23:10

Do you know that in order for gold to be pure it must be heated up to a degree that burns off the impurities and furthermore one of the last things to be burned off and separated from gold is silver. God isn't going for a second place mankind, He wants what is golden. Let me assure you in this, if God has called you to something, He will equip you to succeed in that area. Take a look at Leviticus chapter 19.

"Speak unto all the congregation of the children of Israel, and say unto them, You shall be holy: for I the LORD your God am holy."
-Leviticus 19:2

We are made in His image, and what was possible and expected in the Old Testament is still relevant today. The OT isn't there just as a filler or to round out the Bible, it's there to show us the relationship with Father God, the one that was to be followed and enjoyed from the beginning. Then He gave us Jesus and Jesus sent the Helper, which is the Holy Spirit. We live now in those times, where the Holy Spirit is readily accessible to us and greatly desires to work in our lives. The same spirit, same Holy Spirit that was present at the beginning of Creation and that walked in the garden with Adam & Eve, is the same Spirit which we have with us each day. But I'm getting ahead of myself...

Let's look at this in a different set of terms. Think for a moment if you had a rich uncle (who doesn't want one of those)? Suppose that you found out about this uncle who had untold wealth, the kind that kings & queens have. He has been looking for an heir to take his place because he never had any children of his own, so the nieces and nephews are now in his thoughts to gain the kingdom he has. This kingdom is so vast that it could be shared with you and everyone you ever knew and would still never run out of riches. Now, unfortunately the uncle never finds you and you never find out what wealth and great fortune awaited you and the infinite possibilities of your greatness might not be reached because you are restrained by your limited circumstances. Bummer huh?

You might see already where I'm headed. There is no uncle, but there is One with a Kingdom so vast that the resources could never be exhausted. One that loves you and desires for you to live with Him in all eternity and to share in His riches & glory. You know I am talking about Father God, the One that sent His only Son to bear our sin; Jesus willingly became the ransom for you and & I. We already have the Kingdom within us. For when Jesus says that the Kingdom of God is at hand. This Kingdom is righteousness, peace and joy. The Kingdom is here and what do we do? We keep looking around for more.

It's human nature and I'm going to show you how this same nature in us was around for as long as people have been here to walk the earth.

Absolutely none of what I'm going to show you is by any means meant towards condemnation, rather it is to open your eyes to an age old situation, one that I believe we have the capabilities to resist and to rule over. The result will be a happier and healthier life, one set apart from the aches and pains of the world we live in. Drawing closer to the Creator and partaking in the best that He has to offer us. His Love - unequal to anything else.

Relationships

Relationships with God and with others is very important, God is a generational God and He cares about what things are going on in our families. He has made covenant promises through the generations and He is not a man that He should lie.

I found the information that was tucked away amongst the pages of the Old Testament to be a valuable lifeline like no other.

For 5 years of my life, it seemed that I could not leave the Old Testament, no matter where I started my study, before long I was again roaming around in the old stories and the old problems of the families within.

It was more like "traveling" than studying. I was lost in it all, and I couldn't lay hands on any other thing that gave me so much pleasure as to discover what the Lord purposed for me to find. At first I thought it a sheer coincidence that I saw Jesus in the Old Testament. I mean, it just never occurred to me that He would be hanging out there. By all accounts of what I had been taught growing up, He was in the New Testament.

In about year 2, I got the bright idea to start a catalog of all the places I saw Him popping up. There were prophecies hidden in the old names and the meanings of the names, there were overlays and so many intricacies that I began to doubt I could be seeing what I was seeing! It quickly became evident that to write it all out would amount to rewriting the Old Testament itself. So, even though I thought what I wanted was to know Jesus and the way to achieve that would be to study the Gospels and writings in the New Testament.

What ended up happening was so much better, because God gave me the desire in my heart, He just went about it in a way that I could never have thought up on my own.

Jesus tells us that if you've seen Him, then you've seen the Father. Jesus is a representation of Father God. He states that he does what he has seen the father do. In every way Jesus is obedient and submitted to the will of the Father. Yet, so many of us are fearful and believe that God has a big stick or a lightning bolt with our name on it. That couldn't be further from the truth. I learned that God is just and that He isn't always mad at me. Most people find it easiest to come to Jesus, but Abba -Father Strikes fear in their heart, and the Holy Spirit is considered weird to many folks. These assumptions are red flags in your understanding of the Trinity. I am grateful that I spent those years in the Old Testament because I saw my faults in the ones that came before me, I saw the way that God delivered them and healed them and especially what mountains a repenting heart can lay flat.

I learned that Jesus is my Hope; my anchor of Hope!

I wasn't always so surefooted on my position. In fact I spent far too much time pointing a finger at myself and saying "You aren't good enough!" I thought that God could never accept me because I was one big, giant mess up. You know?

I literally had to drag myself to Him. My inner man had been humbled. The world had beat me up pretty bad and by all accounts I was a filthy mess. My soul was dirty and my spirit was heavy.

I had made every mistake that a woman can make. There was a lot of doubts I had about my condition being restored. It took all the faith I could muster to take that first step.

The Bible says that we are but filthy rags and it didn't take much for me to hit myself over the head with that one! Do you remember being in a season where you knew just enough about the Word to use it against yourself to total destruction. I couldn't keep going on in my own strength with that attitude, I would never have survived my own self-hatred.

Did you ever feel more like the filthy rag that Isaiah describes or the worm that King David calls himself, maybe you felt it was easier to identify with Job when he was at his lowest point in life?

There is a scene in the movie <u>the PASSION of the Christ</u> where Mary Magdalene comes to Jesus.

She is in the most pitiful state, worn out, beat down and ready to give up. What does she find? A loving hand reaching out.

Not judgment, nor condemnation. She isn't told off by Jesus and re-jected. Although I'm sure she thought that any of those things might happen because she was so used to it being the normal response.

I am forever grateful that Jesus saw me for who I am and loved me anyway. That is the kind of love that changes us from the inside out. It washes us clean and sets us on the path we should always have been on. I want you to know that no matter how far gone you think you are, Jesus can find you and He can save you too. All you have to do is call on His name. The name above all names. You can call on Him now, if you never have done so before.

Shift of Focus

One thing I am always looking for and being ever observant of is the change. The change that takes place in the ones I have read about in the Old Testament. I always believed that if someone else did it, then why couldn't I do it also? Sure, some areas of life are limited to talent and natural ability. You won't find me trying to make an album like Celtic Women singing Amazing Grace or building a house like Frank Lloyd Wright. I know my limits. I'm talking about the things that we encounter in the Bible, there are no limits when it comes to faith and the power of God. Actually the boundaries are nonexistent in Christ. With the power of the Holy Spirit working in us and through us we can do what otherwise would be impossible. There is so much power and anointing released in coming through something with Jesus. That is because He is present and working in the situation.

I am ever vigilant to notice the change that takes place when a believer is transformed from here to there.

Look what the meaning of the word encapsulates.

Through is Strong's #5674 and it means to pass over, it is a boundary line; even as in time.

It means to pass over- to overlook; and forgive...
   Through = Cross; as in the Cross of crucifixion.

You don't cross over, unless you are on the shoulders of the only One who can take you over.

> *But now, this is what the Lord says—*
> *he who created you, Jacob,*
> *he who formed you, Israel:*
> *"Do not fear, for I have redeemed you;*
> *I have summoned you by name; you are mine.*
> *2When you pass through the waters,*
> *I will be with you;*
> *and when you pass through the rivers,*
> *they will not sweep over you.*
> *When you walk through the fire,*
> *you will not be burned;*
> *the flames will not set you ablaze.*
> *For I am the Lord your God,*
> *the Holy One of Israel, your Savior;*

I feel much safer going through *with* the Lord than without Him. Look at this version of the same scripture in the [NLT]

> *When you go through deep waters, I will be with you.*
> *When you go through rivers of difficulty, you will not drown.*
> *When you walk through the fire of oppression,*
> *you will not be burned up; the flames will not consume you.*

It can make a difference to read it a second time in a new version. This gives us a deeper understanding of what we will go through and specifically when we are protected.

I can think of several times in my life when I felt like I was on the verge of drowning and Jesus was my life preserver. Have you ever felt like you were going to "burn up" and be consumed by the heat of the troubles you found yourself in?

How do we begin to make the necessary changes? It is true that somethings take time. You spent how long getting into the situation you are in? So, you must allow some time to unravel the mess. I used to picture my problems like spaghetti in a bowl, who could tell where one would even start and where is the end to be found? Overwhelming and a heavy daunting task for sure. I decided to give the bowl of spaghetti to Jesus, I placed the whole thing at His feet. It was time to face the music, I didn't do such a great job "fixing" everything on my own anyway.

He was my last hope, but He was my best hope too.

I began to bring different things to the forefront of my thoughts. This is a terrific place to start, if you just don't know what to do next.

> *Finally, brothers and sisters,*
> *whatever is true,*
> *whatever is noble,*
> *whatever is right,*
> *whatever is pure,*
> *whatever is lovely,*
> *whatever is admirable*
> *—if anything is excellent or praiseworthy—think about such things.*
> *Whatever you have learned or received or heard from me, or seen in*
> *me—put it into practice. And the God of peace will be with you. -*
> *Philippians 4:8-9*

For some, this might be an "easier said than done" kind of thing. No matter who you are though, I bet if you sat down with a pen and journal you could think of one (1) thing for each category listed. Then maybe in time, two (2) things etc. Before you know it, you have quite a list going.

What's next? You take these things into prayer. Yep - you pray as the bible guides us to do. You see, the place you are trying to get to is accessed by "prayer and thanksgiving" Let's look at one scripture that confirms this notion.

"Enter His gates with thanksgiving And His courts with praise. Give thanks to Him, bless His name."-Psalm 100:4

Let me point this out, I know from experience that praise doesn't come easy when you are drowning in your troubles. When each day is a fight just to get out of bed and begin.

That is why I say you start with prayer. Then you bring your list of praises that you took the time to write out in your journal, keeping this journal close by in case it's a real bad day and you can't recall the last time you felt like the sun was shining and the birds were chirping. Here is where the power of God comes in. As you are praying (out of faith) and you are bringing your petitions and your thanksgiving (the journal entries) then the Holy Spirit begins to hover and before you know it, the gates to the "court" open and you are entering... Easily you slip into your attitude of praising because it is natural when you reach that place, moving from the outer courts to the inner courts. Closer to God. We were made to worship. It's supposed to be second nature to us all. But the reality is that it takes some practice and some deliberate restructuring to our daily routines.

This is a big step and a very important one at that. However it is not the only thing to take into account.

New territory comes with new heart attitudes and new mindsets (thoughts, beliefs).

"But you are a chosen race, a royal priesthood, a holy nation, a people for his own possession, that you may proclaim the excellencies of him who called you out of darkness into his marvelous light." -1Peter 2:9

Let's revisit that concept of wanting more... The one I began this chapter with. Suppose that this desire for more was not such an ugly thing. Can we change our perspective just a little now and try looking from the top down, consider that everything God does is good, and towards good.

What if it (our desire for more) were placed there within in each of us from the start. Only the need to satisfy -*were slanted towards* the LORD our God, instead of our flesh. Then the need for more would result in wanting More of God and More of Jesus and our desire could be satisfied in Him. Think about that, isn't our craving for stuff an indication that we feel something is missing? We got it all backwards though and we spend our lives trying to fill the holes in our heart with items made by man. In actuality the only thing that could fill the void is the One who created us with a desire to want more, of HIM. To long for and hope for a deeper relationship. Drawing closer and trusting more, giving our time to Father God instead of the TV or the many other social outlets available.

I never believed that the golden calf was made of gold. When Moses went up the mountain to consult with God and left the people alone for a time (exercising their free will) Well, I just always felt that calf wasn't made of gold after all, it was made of pride. A solution given to themselves, by themselves to immediately gratify their needs. You can see all through-out the pages of the bible, the erroneous decisions made by human kind. We stumble all the time, and God covers us with Mercy & Grace. Why? I believe that His faith in us to come around is because He knows what we are made of and He knows what were are capable of. **Now, if He could just get us to see it also...**

"Trust in him at all times, O people; pour out your heart before him; God is a refuge for us." Selah -Psalm 62:8

Lord, teach me what it means to live a truly grateful life. Help me to "realign" my memories so that I can focus on Your generosity rather than my busy schedule. Bring to my remembrance all that You have done for me and my family, and help me to become that which I cannot become on my own.

In Jesus Name I pray....

Victory in the Blood

The Blood line of Jesus runs through all of us that are saved. As believers, His heritage and what is ours as the heir is for all of us. If Peter could figure it out, then there is hope for all of us. Just like you would do when looking at any family tree, you can begin to see who you are like. Maybe you have a hobby and you discover that there are others who lived before you who shared your love of this craft. You can relate to them, you might even have some of their work that was left behind as a legacy. So much strength and purpose can be gained from this.

We have victory at the cross and in the Blood of Jesus, we are partakers in the inheritance.

Let's rewind a bit. Open up the old box of slides and watch some old home movies for the evening. HA! It isn't difficult for me to play the things over in my mind. It's a little like the idea of the old reel to reel. I can see, hear and even feel things taking place as I read the Word. Just glimpses, but they are so real.

In the block of scripture which I share next, you will be able to see many generations. 14 plus 14 plus another 14 generations to be exact. People lived longer then so it could be a very long span of decades.

I know it's lengthy, but just read it anyway, that will help get you in the flow of where we are going. You will recognize many names along the way. I'm planning on sharing with you just a few of the basics that were significant to me as I began to understand what God was doing by keeping me in the OT. He wanted me to see the way families related to each other and to understand that even when there are major bumbles, HE can still redeem the time and the situations.

The book of the genealogy of Jesus Christ, the Son of David, the Son of Abraham:
2 Abraham begot Isaac, Isaac begot Jacob, and Jacob begot Judah and his brothers. 3 Judah begot Perez and Zerah by Tamar, Perez begot

Hezron, and Hezron begot Ram. **4** Ram begot Amminadab, Amminadab begot Nahshon, and Nahshon
begot Salmon. **5** Salmon begot Boaz by Rahab, Boaz begot Obed by Ruth, Obed begot Jesse, **6** and
Jesse begot David the king.
David the king begot Solomon by her *who had
been the wife*[a] of Uriah.**7** Solomon begot Rehoboam, Rehoboam begot Abijah, and Abijah begot
Asa.[b] **8** Asa begot Jehoshaphat, Jehoshaphat begot Joram, and Joram begot Uzziah. **9** Uzziah
begot Jotham, Jotham begot Ahaz, and Ahaz begot Hezekiah. **10** Hezekiah begot Manasseh,
Manasseh begot Amon,and Amon begot Josiah. **11** Josiah begot Jeconiah and his brothers
about the time they were carried away to Babylon.
12 And after they were brought to Babylon,
Jeconiah begot Shealtiel, and Shealtiel begot
Zerubbabel. **13** Zerubbabel begot Abiud, Abiud
begot Eliakim, and Eliakim begot Azor. **14** Azor
begot Zadok, Zadok begot Achim, and Achim begot Eliud. **15** Eliud begot Eleazar, Eleazar
begot Matthan, and Matthan begot Jacob. **16** And
Jacob begot Joseph the husband of Mary, of
whom was born Jesus who is called Christ.
17 So all the generations from Abraham to David *are* fourteen generations, from David until
the captivity in Babylon *are* fourteen generations, and from the captivity in Babylon until
the Christ *are* fourteen generations.

I won't break them all down in here, but years earlier when my
study began, I did write out all the names and looked into what each
person was up to.

If you have read it, then you know that the bible can read like a
scandalous soap opera at times. I mean, whew! It gets steamy and even
a bit wild. And all of that is still outside of reading Songs of Solomon,
that guy was a true romantic! Most people know him for his intellect,
but let me tell you he was pretty smart around women and I guess if he
figured that mystery out, he should get a prize right there.

I have underlined the ones that I want to share something about.
You can find the beginning of this story in Genesis.

Whenever I do a study in the Good Book I like to just let the Spirit lead me. It's more like traveling than studying and I find that it can be very enlightening because I am open to going wherever it is that the answers are. This means I will not be following the order that scripture is laid out in the bible, rather I will allow the story to unfold as it was given to me. I find it is always most beneficial to read the text before and after a set of scripture being studied. This will enhance the learning and propel you forward at a much faster rate.

That being said, I will only be including some highlights, this will not be an exhaustive case study by any means. It just made me feel like the people that were here before me were genuine, and even with all their flaws on display for the world to read about, they had character, and spunk. These stories show that they were not perfect by any stretch of the imagination, yet they were in the BLOODline of Jesus.

This shows me right off that if they didn't have to be perfect, than I need not place the expectation of perfection upon myself. It is unattainable. No one before or after Jesus was perfect.

I found something though, that each and every one of them did have in common. To discover it was pure joy and the simplicity of it was brilliant. Only God could have pulled this one together, stretched out over 14 generations X's 3 and tucked away within the DNA of all of Jesus ancestors (human).

Well, I won't spoil the ending. Rather I would like to share what I found, in a way that I myself stumbled into the revelation. It's more fun that way, to let the Holy Spirit pull back the curtain and right there before you the unknown and unassuming becomes the pivotal moment in your personal journey.

Keep in mind that I consider all of the people in the bible, and in the lineage of Jesus to be my family. Yes, I think on them like long distant relatives that I never met, only I share a bond with them because we are in the same family and that is by the Salvation of Christ. If you are born again, you can think of these people the same way. I found great comfort in that because my earthly parents have been deceased many years, more than twenty for my mother and there is the foster homes I bounced around to and from like a ping-pong ball. Not much in the way of family ties there. I do talk to one family still, but they live in the town where so much pain and confusion took place, that spending time with them there is torture.

So I allowed the Lord to be my family and as I got to know the ones from the pages I read every day, they became very real to me. I laughed with them and I cried with them and they imparted their words of wisdom to me, which guided my life. Isn't that family? I mean, sure I know Peter isn't really related to me, but doesn't everyone have an overbearing, loud mouthed uncle that means well and has a big heart even though he puts his foot in his mouth more often than not? Can't we all think of a Mary or a Martha in our families of today? Even in our churches, aren't those folks your family too? So, indulge me for a bit and who knows, maybe you would realize that you just might have found yourself out camping with Jacob and using a rock for a pillow. Who can say?

What's in a Name?

Jacob, is one person in the Bible that did not escape my attention, talk about having ups and downs in life. If you like to read about your favorite villain and your favorite underdog who gets it figured out in the end, becoming one of the Patriarchs in Jesus linage, then you would want to follow the life of Jacob.

Talk about turning things around! I admit, that I was disgusted by this whole family when I began reading it, I was shocked and confused at how they were in here at all? So many mistakes and such ugliness was in their hearts. But, they were real people and they were given real opportunities to change and to walk in the light of Who God is. They were offered Salvation, in the form that was available before Jesus came to us as the son of man. Amazing life changes, nothing could wring my heart more than to find my own self mirrored in their lives. Not to the end result of anger and frustration, but instead to the saving grace of forgiveness at the feet of Jesus. I disliked them, and I loved them and I found answers and instruction for my own life from within their lives. The Old Testament is just that, it is the oldest testimony to God's goodness and redemptive love that was given to mankind.

Jacob wrestled with the Lord for nearly all of his life. Literally from the womb and into his adulthood. At every turn you can see the path that he followed was directly relevant to the upbringing from his mother's devious plots and his father's lack of involvement and indifferent attitudes. Jacob and Esau had parents that played favorites. Each one had their own plight and each had to figure out the correct way to live life, but not without losing a whole lot along the way. Neither one of them had "family" close by. They split off and lived separately. Jacob ended up losing touch with his mother, the one person he was closest too growing up. All the lying and cheating caught up to him and he felt the sting of it. Deceit came back around to him time and time again. Yet, the people in the OT knew something that we have forgotten about, they knew God was real. They don't tell stories about the doubts they had of God's existence, they tell stories of the doubts about the enormity of the miracles He will perform. Even they were amazed and found the size of God's limits to be limitless. But they never doubted or questioned His very existence as so many do today. I'm saying that there weren't atheists and apostasy was not in the Bloodline of Jesus. And I can show you.

There are two significant times in Jacob's life that I really could relate to. One is found in the dream that he had (Genesis 28) Jacob is traveling home, I always wondered if he felt the dread that I did when the Lord asked me to return "full circle" to the town I left after my husband ended his life in suicide. I had many dreams and even a few visions as I was working things out in my heart and even in my mind, because some of the things that happened were really hard to believe in the natural and only did they make any sense at all when placed against the spiritual realm.

The second is found more in depth in (Genesis 32-38) when God gives Jacob his new name. I could identify so much with this Patriarch of the Bible, he knew what it felt like to want to belong and to do whatever was necessary to find a place to fit in.

Jacob had parental "issues" but so did his father Isaac, and so did Abraham. You can see it come down the line. Abraham left his family, he was instructed to by the LORD. That right there in those times was a huge step of faith. People nowadays move all over and barely bat an eye. Abraham's family worshiped the moon and moon gods. This was an area that the LORD wanted to pull Abraham out of and to build (form) the new covenant line away from such beliefs. God wanted a people that loved and feared Him (feared, as in a reverent and respectful way, like I know He is God so I take Him seriously)

Every time Abraham moved he built an altar (to the LORD) and he dug a well. I won't go into all the significance that (well) holds, maybe I will leave that for you to search out, but let yourself think for a moment if you were 'following' Abraham...Remember he is the first one mentioned and he is the 1st Patriarch and he was the original one that God made the covenant with.

Isaac and Rebekah played favorites. So did Abraham. They did not hide their love for a "special and unique" child. Today, we try to make every one equal. That was not the way in OT times. If you had a calling or an anointing on your life then you were treated differently. So different that your brothers jealousy would rather have you sold into slavery than to put up with you, as this did happen to Joseph (Genesis 37) If you have heard the story then you know that Joseph was Jacob's favorite son born to him by Rachel (the wife he was tricked out of marrying).

So much treachery, and so much redemption. If you could ever see how much the LORD works things out to good, it would be through the life of Jacob and his offspring. Sometimes it takes more than one generation to iron out the kinks.

Isaac was a "favorite child" and he in turn had his favorite too. Esau was that boy. Only you do not find Esau mentioned in the passage I showed you to illustrate the genealogy of Jesus Christ. You find his twin brother, Jacob. There is a good reason for this, and we find it in the story of Esau trading his birthright to Jacob for a bowl of red stew. The original idea was from Rebekah (the boy's mother) Jacob plots to make this deal, but in the end Esau is guilty of letting go of the most precious thing he had, his place as first born.

Before you think it too dastardly on Jacobs part, let me point out that his own father (Isaac) took hold of his place as first born and the rights and privileges therein by a bit of double-dealing as well. This story would most likely hold a lot of bitterness on the side of Ishmael, who was the first born of Abraham, yet he and his mother were sent away into the wilderness. God did not forget about Ishmael, even if Abraham seemingly cast him aside.

The point I am bringing up is that no matter what the troubles this family had, there was one very strong thread that kept running through each of them. It was the thread of Faith. They believed in God and did not question Him.

As for Esau and Jacob, they did make amends after fourteen long years of separation. That is what happens when the pain is too great to deal with and we do it still today, we run and we avoid those that have caused us the pain.

None of the things Jacob went after ever came easy to him. He wanted and coveted his brother's birthright, and I believe that God allowed the exchange to happen because if you read the story, all parties in one way or another agreed to it. So much so that even when Isaac knew what had happened he gave into it and trusted that the LORD would work it out. Everyone involved trusted in the LORD, and in the end He did work it out.

This next scripture is truly amazing to me. I found so much hope in it for my own life.

He said, "Your name shall no longer be Jacob, but Israel; for you
have striven with God and with men and have prevailed."
-Genesis 32:28

If you're not sure who it is that Jacob is wrestling with, it is the angel of the LORD, and whenever you see this written you can know that it is Jesus who is spoken of here.

When this exchange took place, many long years later after all that I just wrote about and so much more it is written that Jacob "prevailed". This does not mean that his way won out over God's way. Rather, something so much more beautiful has taken place. Jacob has finally learned to humble himself and to submit to God's plan for his life. The exchange is marked forever by Jesus changing his name from Jacob (which meant liar) and would now be Israel (meaning in the Hebrew KJV: **Israel: for as a prince hast thou power.**)

Could you imagine, that all your life you were known as a liar and deceiver? Named so at birth, you were the supplanter of your own destiny. Maybe it's not such a surprise to see that he lived it out.

I found it difficult to relate to Jacob for all his lying set me on edge. It always seemed easier to deal in the truth, but I know now that is because of the seer gift that I have and didn't always know what to do with.

Aside from the lies, I was able to relate to Jacob because I will never forget the striving that went on between myself and the Lord Jesus. I will always remember the scripture He gave me and revealed to me my name and its meaning. See Revelations 2:17

"He who has an ear, let him hear what the Spirit says to the churches. To him who overcomes, to him I will give some of the hidden manna, and I will give him a white stone, and a new name written on the stone which no one knows but he who receives it."

There is so much information in that one scripture! ...to him who overcomes: as you know by now, if you are reading this series it is evident that I had some obstacles to get over in my life. Like Jacob, my struggle for significance began at the womb and it did not change until I began the walk of true humility and submitting my will to the will of God.

At a later date, I plan to do a full teaching on the hidden manna, for now let it suffice to say that most of the revelations that I share along the way are just that, they are the hidden manna. It is the holy food that the saints get to take part in as they are fed from the fount of all Life.

When all of this took place it was at the same time of moving away from Alaska and back to the place I was running from, the place where my husband had died by suicide and we left in order to begin again to try and have a normal life. One that could be free of snide remarks and judgmental stares that condemned you as a murderer. How very unkind the Catholic Church was to us, and severe was their rejection. It really was unfair to assume that everything would be exactly as it had been when I left. Instead the Lord placed us in a new church and a whole different evangelical attitude was more the lead. It was a place of new beginnings.

As I was preparing to leave Alaska I asked the Lord why I had to go back there to this place of death and sadness. He told me the scripture in Rev 2:17 **"a white stone, and a new name".**

There were things in that place which I still had to "overcome" and there was a huge learning curve. I grew so much spiritually while I was there. I believe that it was through those difficult and triumphant times that I was sharpened and prepared for the biggest battle that I had yet to face. What I didn't know then was that my son Justin David would die as his father David died, by taking his own life too. That story is coming in <u>Scars of Suicide</u>.

I always had the name Patricia, what I did not have and grew to love was the meaning of the name. Just like Jacob, the Lord gave me my new name, with a new understanding. Patricia means Victorious and Overcomer! That is how amazing God is, He knew who I was called to be, no matter if I felt the opposite.

For all my life and up until that day in May of 2007 only days before I left the last frontier I chose every variation of the name Patricia that I could come up with. Including different spellings and even Pepper was used briefly. The attitude was to begin anew. To wipe the slate clean and start over. What I came to learn was that only Jesus has the power to do such a thing and there never was a way for me to accomplish this on my own. Yet, I tried and that story was written out of faith and given into God's hands immediately after I arrived back in the place I dreaded so much. The Lord took that story and published it in two separate editions and took it to 107 Nations and translated those books into 6 languages. I couldn't believe it, should someone in

Pakistan really need to know of my seriously lopsided self-hatred? Well, I don't argue the point, I just trust that He knows what He is doing.

Generational Lord

In all of this family history, I do hope that you are seeing the way that God works in and through people's lives. This matters a great deal because even now thousands of years later we get caught in the trap of thinking that nothing will ever change for us. Maybe we feel trapped by a negative label that was placed upon our family or even upon us individually. It can be hard to shake free of these types of labels. Let's look at a few more instances from the 1st book of the Bible and see what the covenant family is up to now.

Judah is one such example of living in the shadow of greatness. He never really felt special and he never acted quite right either. Still, the Lord sets it straight and draws out the strength that is within Judah.

Judah is Jacob's boy, born of Leah and not Rachel (as Joseph was) Jacob's favorite wife bore his favorite sons. The irony here is that Rachel dies, and all the children are raised by Leah. Once again you will see some shifting of birth rights. Joseph is the one who gets the birthrights and not either of his older brothers Reuben or Judah.

However the lineage of Jesus Christ comes down through one of Judah's twin sons, Perez. -Thus fulfilling this prophesy:

"All the families of the earth shall be blessed" -Matthew 1:3, 16.

How in the world does that happen? This is where things get a bit scandalous! Judah marries a Canaanite woman, remember that up to this point the men in his family were avoiding doing just this. The belief systems were not the same as Abraham, Isaac and Jacob. With that in mind, realize how the mama of the children is going to instill her beliefs, and produce a different kind of offspring. Here is what happened to her children and a glimpse of how they were as men. The full story is in Genesis 38.

Judah took a wife, Tamar, for his firstborn son, Er, but he was so evil that God took his life. Judah commanded his second-born son, Onan, to marry Tamar and produce an heir for his deceased brother as God's laws commanded in such circumstances. Onan would not carry through with this act because it would not be his heir. God then took Onan's life for his refusal to give his brother an heir -
Genesis 38:8-10

The story goes on to tell how Tamar plays a harlot (casting her in a bad light) she ends up pregnant. Judah is enraged because he told Tamar to wait until his 3rd son was grown and then she could have children with that guy. Well, this doesn't happen because Judah was lying all along. Finally his wife dies and he is going on a trip. That is when Tamar fools him into having a little fling up in the cave. She ends up having Judah's twin boys!

When the twins are born you see the same behavior as Jacob's trickery with his brother.

At delivery, one twin put out his hand first and the midwife tied a scarlet thread on it and said, "This one came out first." But the other twin, Perez, came out unexpectedly followed by Zerah with the scarlet thread tied on his hand
-Genesis 38:27-30

Once again God honors what has taken place. Perez will be in the direct line of David the King and of course later on, Jesus. There can be seen a great amount of family loyalty here and strong Faith in God. It did not escape my attention that the faithless were removed and not allowed to reproduce. Tamar was faithful to Judah's family, even though he nearly ended the family lineage and would have broken the promise in his negligence. God did not allow that to happen, He guards his promise to Abraham. I just love that part. Furthermore, Judah ends up with two boys in place of the two he lost. God brings righteousness into a not so right world.

It is the pure line of Faith that I hope you saw manifest itself through God's chosen family. Their strength and loyalties will carry on down to the Lamb of God. This is the very thing that so strongly impressed itself upon me. There were none, not one person in the line of Jesus that did not have Faith! This same Blood runs through you because you are saved and washed in the sanctified Blood of the sacrificial Lamb, who was slain on the cross for the remission of sin. Only the Blood of Jesus can take away the sins of the world.

Internal Battle to Believe

What a conflict raging in me. I had given my life to Jesus, and I meant it. Yet, for a few seasons, my prayer life seemed like I kept repeating the process. When we find salvation, our transformation is a Holy moment and no devil can stop this transaction. However, there are plenty of folks who still beat themselves up, and walk around filled with doubts concerning their salvation experience. I heard a Pastor talk about it once, with 40 years under his ministry belt he never forgot how the devil tried to trick him into thinking he didn't really, actually, truly get saved. So, what is going on in this area of indecisiveness?

I visualize the old sin like trash. In our salvation experience we are pulled to Christ when we give Him our hearts, but there is still a magnitude of gunk left behind, likened to a residual of a bad smell, even if you remove the offending source. Let there be no doubt when Jesus removes our sin, He says it is buried in the ocean and as far removed as the east is from the west.

He will turn again, he will have compassion upon us; he will subdue our iniquities; and thou wilt cast all their sins into the depths of the sea. Micah 7:19

Imagine taking out the trash, but the stench of it still lingers. This lingering odor is the exact thing the enemy is attracted to. It's like a trail back to you remaining long after you get saved. Unless you begin to deal with your old stinky trash right away. Need an example? Not forgiving another person (including yourself). Well, why not start with this one?

Things get amped up for instances of suicide, because you have many "stinky" areas all at once. The short list is guilt, anger, depression and possibly the fear of death. You know how an animal can sense fear? Put it in this context for any area that you struggle with. Following a suicide, the spirit of death is extremely strong and can be so severe that the spirit of suicide clings to these areas of your life and fuels your own doubts about your very existence or the need for you to continue your life. The whispers circle around your head saying, "Nobody cares anyway if you are dead or alive."

You wonder where the taunting voices come from, and how can they gain power to harass you this way? Why won't it just leave you alone? Because, as I clearly spelled out in the Lies we believe, you aren't doing anything to stop it, and you are in fact enabling the demonic nuisances to continue, by agreeing with them. How do we "agree" with it? Any time you say the negative back to yourself you are agreeing with the father of lies, who comes only to steal, kill and destroy you and your life.

This is the part nobody wants to deal with.

They say, "I am saved, why would all these bad things still be happening to me?" May I suggest it's because of this "odor" that the enemy identifies you as someone he can harass? These are the things you must work through. So begins the process of walking out your Salvation. You see, when you invited Jesus to live in your heart, He came in willingly. In my instance He had to squeeze into a very cramped space because my heart was already full. Containing countless grievances against others, and many more towards myself. As I learned the Word and began to apply it to my daily life, the Lord, then began to help me remove my trash, once and for all. I could literally feel a difference in being ready to let go.

I can't precisely count the exact number of times I kept giving my heart to Jesus, but I marvel that He would take every offense I offered up and scrape it clean. My cry echoed from the Psalms "Create in me a clean heart, O God and renew in me a right spirit," I think I allowed various Psalms to become the source of most of my cries, finding in them a way to express what I simply had no words for. The books of Samuel aided in this task as well. Letting go means you do not pick it back up again.

My Salvation process didn't need to be repeated, but the heart cry accompanying it did. A spirit of repentance and the surrendering; when the Lord brings you low enough to see what is actually down in the bottom. The truth of your anguish is most likely buried below years of excuses and tactics to dodge and avoid the pain. The better you have become at hiding from the pain, the longer it may take to come face to face with it.

I finally learned and understood my position in Christ was secure, and in fact my attitude of repentance could come as needed without sweeping me out of eternity every time I hit another snag. For a long time I was a "double minded man", meaning I didn't believe all the scriptures applied to me. I still carried a grudge against the person closest to me... ME. There is a real danger of getting caught here. Such a place of vacillating is no place for a born again Christian. How many of us get stuck here? This is where my strongest call to action came. My heart for ministry is based in this process of repentance and forgiveness. The end result is a deeper walk and a closer relationship with the Holy Trinity.

Scripture clearly tells us the double- minded man is unstable in all his ways. I did not sin in the part that I was unsure of my identity in Christ, I am a disciple and always learning. Let's face it, some scripture is so life changing it can take years of meditation to allow it to take root. There is a Sovereign flow to the Lord's ways. You find that He takes you quickly to new heights and other times the steps drag on. During these times I always see an image of me dragging my feet. These movements in the Spirit Realm are like waves, and the tides. All moving at God's Perfect Will. You could no more speed up the coming tide than you could speed up the process of change in your heart. The Lord knows the rhythm of your heart and at the speed in which you can comprehend the Thoughts of Heaven.

The human error comes in the area of Faith. I think so many come to Christ, and they are sincere and love the Lord. Yet, patience wears thin and it starts to take too long for the process of getting to "a good place". Wouldn't it just be easier to just do what we have always done? That is when Faith must to take over and keep us moving forward. Ever forward in the Lord, He only has one direction and that is on to the next level. Upward.

We move forward and He draws us Upward. Faith can destroy any tactic of the enemy, from anxiety to zealousness. Faith is in Him, and He can do anything. He also has faith in our ability to succeed through Him. Because He knows who He is, even if we are still struggling with certain Truths. He is part of us, therefore we are enabled to accomplish the impossible.

Because of these things a position of "double-mindedness" can't work in the Saints. Remember, if you believe one thing the Bible says, you should believe all that it tells us. Every word. Especially the ones that are difficult. These are the ones Jesus works through with the greatest power. How? He can because you have the best chance of success if you join Him in your transformation. He won't force you, but He will come in and smash all the plans of the enemy as soon as you call upon Him and then step aside. By this I mean, you can't ask Him to do {fill in the blank} and then stand there and tell Him how to go about getting those things done. You must allow Him to take the lead and to remain in the lead. I have a tendency to run ahead of the Lord, so I know this behavior can cause some setbacks when we do take off full tilt with only half the information. I mean seriously, did I ever really think He needed me to point the way? I was naive. The good news is, He was always right where I left Him to run off on my own. His patience is the thing to win me over. Oh, what love is in that patience as He waits for me to understand within my soul. Is there anything better than that moment when God touches you and a true connection and an everlasting understanding are infused within your very fiber?

During a worship service called 'Audience of One' I experienced an amazing encounter with the Lord. I use this experience as a benchmark now to remind myself, just how far I've traveled with King Jesus.

The whole evening was centered on worshiping Our Creator. This was not a church service per say, the purpose was to draw close to the fire of the Lord. I was always so excited to come to any Praise gathering because these are my favorite times with the Lord. One I mimic at home as well. Soaking Prayer, the portal to Heaven.

I was deliberately positioned in another place in the sanctuary from where I stood during regular Sunday service. The music played on for over an hour. Some prophetic words were given and I listened with awe to the voice of Heaven flowing through these servants of God.

All of a sudden I saw a light, I reached up towards the light, it was really bright and I wanted to touch it, place my hand closer. Odd as it sounds I felt love for this light. So I kept staring, not wanting it to go away. I remember that the sight of this light made me giggle out loud, before I caught myself, afraid of being heard. Then I told the Lord (from my heart) I loved the light I saw and I said "What is this Lord? Is that you?" So beautiful, so, so Beautiful!

He said " The light is you, Patricia"

His reply was simple yet, it shook me to the core.

"HUH?" what? You're kidding!?

He was showing me, how *He* saw me. I tell you, I was surprised! But then I felt Him reach down inside of me and something "clicked" I felt it move, like a piece being snapped into place inside a puzzle. My DNA was moved around. I know how it sounds to the world outside of this realm, but I'm telling you the truth of what happened. Did He remove something or add some things? Perhaps both.

I now had to accept this new truth. But how would I do that without letting go of the old truth, the one I had been wearing around like an old ratty garment?

Repeating the process of repentance and accepting cleansing have become a lifestyle for me, trading my double minded thoughts for the thoughts of a Holy God. When I started to memorize scripture I had a bad habit of using those words against myself. This is when I would recognize the enemy and the evidence of his foul play in my life. One day, after years of this, the Lord told me to draw a cross on a piece of paper. So, in my overzealous attitude of showing Him how much I loved Him, I drew a great big cross on yellow legal paper.

Big 3-D like and I set it on a hill too. *smile* "Like this Lord?"

[He instructed me to write all the things that I knew in the scriptures which were places I had identified myself. He said put the negative ones on the left and on the right place the ones that are good and holy.]

Oh, dear. This proved to be an exhausting task. My mind over-flowed with all the things I was certain were against me. I identified with Rahab and Jacob before he was Israel and all the times King David drug himself through the mud. Can you imagine, even scripture about the devil got on the legal paper, how he was a liar and everything nasty every person in the Bible had done wrong I took it for my own and it went on the left side. The Old Testament and the new poured out. The whole page was crammed with bible references to the ugliest things mankind ever did. I thought "This is who I am." Adding up all the mis-takes because I had made so many and I wanted to show the Lord just why I didn't belong in Heaven with Him. How could He want some-thing so disgusting as me in a place of so much beauty?

And that was it! The real thing which we found on the bottom of my barrel when I went scrapping around with the Lord. I believed that I didn't belong among the Blessed and that I could only defile that which was Holy. I believed that I was too damaged, possibly evil too, even though I wanted so much to be counted among the righteous. This is a double-mind, and it had to go. None of the slanderous things I believed about myself were anywhere close to the good thoughts which God had towards me.

These are the words Jesus spoke to my heart when I discovered all this to be my truth. He told me to take one last look at that list of wrongs I had against myself and he said this "I have already taken all that away, when I hung on the Cross and by my stripes you are healed." He continued... "Never again my daughter are you to hold these offenses against yourself, for I have taken them away."

Decision time. In that moment I knew I was free, and that all the years of hatred and guilt were being swept away, I didn't feel like re-sisting anymore. I was exhausted at all the fighting to keep unforgiveness against myself. If I wanted to let it go, I could.... So I fought all the things inside that wanted to cling to the old ways and I pushed those out. Out of my mind and out of my heart. My slate was clean. I will spend the rest of my life resisting the devil on this issue. He still comes around in times of trouble to begin his whispering. But I focus on the face of Jesus and I ask Him to help me stay the course.

With every chapter of this book, the enemy appeared. He kept taunting me, who are you to write a book about God?

I would look at the face of Jesus (held in my heart and mind) and I would see Him, He smiles back and says "Who are you, not too?"
Indeed.

During prayer ministry, I hear a lot of "I can't" and "I shouldn't"...
Many believe they are *unworthy* and *unwelcome* before the throne of God.

I understand, I used to have those thoughts too. Once upon a time, when I knew the bare minimums about Jesus or a love that stretches beyond the expanse of the known universe.

It breaks my heart, because nothing could be further from the truth.

What can you do then? You are faced with two choices and only one of them brings you into eternal life. If you follow the world, then you will go as the world goes.

"A blind man cannot guide a blind man, can he? Will they not both fall into a pit...?" -Luke 6:39

When all else fails and you cannot find the answers to your situation and gain a personal insight, you must always follow the plumbline. The straight course, the builder's line to the foundation.

Even when faced with certain death and in the final hours of His life, Jesus surrendered His will and chose the Father's perfect plan for His life. And that was to save us all from an eternal damnation, forever separated from God.
As my final thoughts on the matter, I would like to look at a scripture out of 1Corinthians 13:4-7
Remember that God is love.

Change the word "love" to God and you start to see Him in a new light!

Love is patient,
love is kind.
It does not envy,
it does not boast,
it is not proud.
It does not dishonor others,
it is not self-seeking,
it is not easily angered,
it keeps no record of wrongs.
Love does not delight in evil but rejoices with the truth.
It always protects, always trusts, always hopes, always perseveres.
...love never dies
~1Corinthians 13:8

A "New Way" of Looking at an Old Problem

I used to pray that I would never "lose" my deepest desire to know the Lord. I remember when I was a brand new Christian and I would get little glimpses of God, they delighted me so much but I would panic that He would leave, that I would "mess it up" and then my time would be gone forever. Silly as it seems now, that was my thought process. I would get up around 6 am to spend time in the Word before my children awoke for school. At that time I had 1 teen in middle school and an elementary 3rd grader along with a two year old toddler and an infant. Quiet time was a rare item and I did what I could, knowing that God understood my situation and desire for more.

Fast forward to present day as I pull these materials together, to share my tools of warfare with all that choose to take my recommendations.

The babies are about to turn 14 & 12. My desire has only increased as I now get up at 3:20 am so that I will be in the prayer place by 4:00am. I get more time for worship (which opens the court gates) and I freely move around the tabernacle, eating and partaking of the goodness of God. I am living in such a place of peace it brings me to tears when I think on it. I am grateful for what the Lord provided to me all these years and the ability to walk with Him in all that He had to show me. What generosity!

While on my journey through many fires, I came to realize a few shocking things about the Lord. He does challenge us, but it's for the growth that comes from the sifting, the pruning, the purging and the fire which burns off the dross.

In all seasons I can look back on now and see that His hand was surely with me, and that He too was in fact, right in the flames as I was in the flames.

> *"When you go through deep waters, I will be with you. When you go through rivers of difficulty, you will not drown. When you walk through the fire of oppression, you will not be burned up; the flames will not consume you." ~Isaiah 43:2*

This is one of the "old problems" I want to address. To gain victory you must decide (in your heart) as I decided in my own heart is God for me or is He against me? This cannot be decided with your logic, it must come from your inner chamber. Why is this an issue, you might wonder.

Because let's face it, when trouble comes we say things like "Why did God let this happen?" or "Where was God when blank & blank took place."

Death and especially death in a violent way will stir these questions within us.

Many times over the years as I was able to pray with others I began to see patterns, first they were like flags that warned of danger, the danger they were in and a nearby pitfall (but I did not yet see with love as my spyglass) and many times my warnings came across as judgments.

Then these flags were clearly becoming reflections of my own heart, with things such as unforgiveness and the Lord would use their hearts to make me look at my own heart too. Like a check-up or a tune- up. I nearly bolted a few times for the sheer vulnerability that it took to continually examine my heart before I could even utter one word of prayer for another. Hours upon hours did I rend my heart. He has a way of humbling us and fixing us at the same moment.

In time these evidences of the enemy -well, they began to look more like a beaten down path. A path that I had long since abandoned, but could see (as the Lord allowed) my brother or sister walking along the path to unseen danger, snags and traps set by the enemy.

Having been shown the unmeasurable love of Jesus towards me, I knew that each person was so loved by Him as well and that He lay His life down for each one, for the purpose that all could know the Unfailing Love of the Father.

He uses our heart as a mirror.

First we only see other's faults in the reflection and eventually we begin to see ourselves and our faults in the reflection, until the day that we can only see Christ. To me that is the process of walking out Salvation.

The same "old problem" is also rooted in the sins of our hearts (no matter how they got there) and the activity of the enemy in our everyday lives.

I will explain further, because these are hard pills to swallow.

Not one of us gets through this life without some kind of trouble. Just take a look at the disciples of Jesus, they lived with the Master and you might think that they died a hero's death. Parades given honoring the work they did for the love of the Lord. Yet if you were to look into it further (as I did one morning) you would see horror and terror in their deaths. No parades and no flowers nor any memorials set up for them. Dying in their faith was their true badge of honor. What I saw in their deaths was that only one thing really matters while we are here on planet earth and that is to come to know the Lord Jesus Christ. If you are given an opportunity to work out any ugliness in your heart and be purified here and now before you leave for the eternal resting place, then the Bible says you are pretty fortunate!

I am no stranger to the trials of life, but I was a stranger to the saving grace of God to help me out of my various plights. I did not understand the whiles of the devil or the enormous amount of mercy available to me as I figured out what trickery I had been victim too. Yes, I was tricked by people that I should have been able to trust, and I was duped by figures in authority that never should have abused their position of power. These things made it difficult to trust the supreme authority that God has over my life. Yet, even as I was injured and innocence lost as a child, I had to find the way back to God through the purity of a child's heart, one who believes without condition in the Holiness and Sovereign place rightfully owed by Father God.

He showed me the triggers that pulled me out of my place of safety with Him. He showed me the Strongman and the tactics of the way the enemy uses multiple areas of your life to make you feel defeated and hopeless. Have you ever felt like the "deck was stacked" against you? That is exactly how the devil operates and once you find out your authority to remove him from your life, you will no longer be left feeling bullied, nor helpless.

Prayer Portions

I pray that you are girded up and filled with the fortitude it takes to find the Freedom *IN* Christ that awaits you. Do not lose sight of the fact that Jesus died on the cross so that you would not have to live in condemnation. All the words and offenses that you hold against yourself, they must become a thing of the past and remain in your past.

Now, the journey for you might just be starting, but I pray you will allow it to take place in your life. Nobody ever regrets the first steps of believing they can be better tomorrow, than they were today.

If you identified any "doors" or negative entry points from your own life write them down and take them into prayer, just as I have shown you to do.

I am so honored to be any part of your healing. You can have a future filled with Hope and Love. It is possible to find the same treasures that I found and I pray now that you receive them to the full measure. May the Lord Bless you, as you continue to press into the High Calling.

...And they stood together as a great witness to the faithfulness and redeeming love of their Lord Jesus.

ABOUT THE AUTHOR

Patricia King is a 20th Century Deborah, strong in faith, rooted in Christ, with the stamina of a modern day warrior. On the Journey to Healing, Patricia reaches out to others who have been affected by the trauma of suicide, reinforces the value and beauty of life, and ushers the oppressed into the presence of God.

Through God's grace, Patricia founded the Scars of Suicide ministry online, in an effort to reach the four corners of the earth for Jesus. Her message of love is evidenced as she pushes back the taboo of suicide to witness to a hurting people, where suicide is no respecter of persons. Her transparency not only ministers hope to others, but it also ushers her into a place of spiritual rest too, a place she believes is possible for all God's children.

She resides in Upstate New York with her husband and 3 children.

For Inner Healing Worksheets & Personal Ministry
Contact Author at:
www.scarsofsuicide.com

www.ingramcontent.com/pod-product-compliance
Lightning Source LLC
Chambersburg PA
CBHW061735020426
42331CB00006B/1251